UNLOCKING THE
TRUTH of DANIEL

DIGGING DEEPER SERIES (BOOK ONE)

UNLOCKING THE
TRUTH of DANIEL

LAURA J. DAVIS

REACH ONE PUBLISHING

LONDON, ONTARIO

Dedicated to My Mother, Who Taught Me How to Pray

ACKNOWLEDGMENTS

It is impossible to create a book if you do not listen to the helpful advice of others. So, I want to thank my Beta Readers Janis Cox, Carol Roch, Sylvia and Jeff Balch, and Barbara Derksen. Your comments and suggestions were instrumental in shaping this book.

Of course, no book ever gets finished without an editor and I am fortunate to have one of the best. Thank you, Stephanie Nickel. What would I do without you?

A special thank you to my daughter Sarah Anne Davis, who designed my book cover. Can I get you to do all my covers from now on?

Finally, to all those who read my books, thank you for reading them and for stopping by my blog with your comments. Thank you for the encouraging cards and emails. I love hearing from you.

CONTENTS

"Do your best to present yourself to God as one approved, a worker who has no need to be ashamed, rightly handling the word of truth."

—2 Timothy 2:15

FOREWORD

Do the images and prophecies contained in the Old Testament Book of Daniel intrigue you and yet you're uncertain as to how you might figure out what is past or present or maybe future? Laura J. Davis' *Unlocking the Truth of Daniel* study may be just what you need.

She patiently leads her students through the Scriptures and a maze of historical detail spanning centuries. Repeat mention of certain events, personages and dynasties, along with helpful charts keep students in touch with where the study has taken them and aids in their progression.

Laura ably employs the inductive Bible study method and in the process facilitates the student in adopting that approach in a natural, conversational way. I am certain that learning, discovery and growth will occur for many who faithfully work their way through this study. Investments of thought, prayer, and effort will be rewarded.

I have no hesitation in recommending *Unlocking the Truth of Daniel* for either private or group study.

This work is rich in historical background and fascinating in detail, and is also far-reaching in implication. Brace yourself though, for on occasion, Laura challenges widely-held cherished notions about "end times," making her case cogently where that occurs. Important, however, is that she urges students to prayerfully do some digging of their own, and not to simply take her word for it.

Laura J. Davis, with a true heart, demonstrates strong resolve and steady commitment to searching out the truths of God's Word, in this the first book in her Digging Deeper Series.

— Rev. Peter A. Black (retired), columnist and author of
Parables From the Pond and
Raise Your Gaze...Mindful Musings of a Grateful Heart

PREFACE

When I became a Christian some thirty plus years ago, one of the things that attracted me the most was reading my Bible. You may think that is the same for everyone who becomes a Christian. True. But did you make your non-believing friends sit down in your dining room and read the Bible with you? Out loud? I was seventeen and a first class Bible thumper. I shudder to think about it now and hope I didn't impede my friends from eventually finding God.

Fast forward through the years and one of the things that continued to stick with me was my love of the Scriptures. I would often have Bible studies in my home and loved to share (with whoever would listen) what I had learned. Still, I felt something was missing during my study times. I wanted to dig a little deeper and God knew it. Before long I was introduced to a concept called inductive Bible study through Precept Ministries, led by Kay Arthur. After attending one of her conferences, I could feel my spirit yearning to get back home and crack open my Bible to put my new-found skills to work. Little did I know that God was preparing me for better things. By the end of the conference, I wanted to be one of those who would go out and teach others how to study the same way, and I prayed that one day it would be possible. On the last day of the conference, my prayer was answered when a friend informed me she had signed me up and paid for me to get the proper training. All I needed to do was pay for the hotel for the three-day event. I was over the moon! But the inductive studies of Precept Ministries required homework (at least an hour a day) and one meeting a week to go over that homework. I began to realize people either didn't have the time to study or they just weren't interested enough to invest the time necessary. I became resigned to having the training and no one to share it with.

That was then. With the advance of the internet and social media, sharing what God is showing me during my study times is now just a mouse click away. But sometimes a little more is needed than a blog and books are born.

This study of Daniel took me close to a year because it involved an enormous amount of historical research. Thus, what you are about to read is a combination of inductive study, keeping the Scriptures in context, and historical research. The underlying question for me as I progressed was this: why didn't the Jews view Daniel's prophecies with the end-times in mind while Christians did? There was a reason they saw him as a minor prophet. I hope this study will bring you closer to understanding why.

INTRODUCTION

Welcome to this study of the book of Daniel. This is the first book in the Digging Deeper Series, designed to help you find hidden truths in scripture that may have puzzled you for years. If this is your first time studying Daniel, I am sure you will find it both inspiring and exciting. Daniel was a man of faith who lived an obedient life to God. Yet he managed to gain the respect and admiration of those who did not share his beliefs. As Christians increasingly come under persecution for their beliefs, Daniel's life will be an example for us to follow.

However, the book of Daniel provides us with so much more than "life lessons." In it, we find prophecies that have already been fulfilled and others that are still in our future. Who are the kings of the north and south and what role do they play in the end-times? While many speculate on who they might be, this study will guide you to the truth using the Scriptures and history as our guides.

Getting Started

Besides Daniel's inspiring faith, this book is both historical and prophetic. So we will approach this study in context with history and scripture. We will look at it verse by verse, making use of why, when, where, how, what, and who questions.

If you are doing this alone, you can do a chapter each day or take it at your own pace. In a group setting, the facilitator should decide which chapters to complete each week. If you get stuck, there is an answer key in the back of this book as well as a facilitator's guide.

How to Use This Study in a Group Setting

It is always best to appoint a facilitator for your group. A facilitator is not a teacher but rather someone who keeps the discussion on track and on time. Not every question needs answering. Some may prove more time consuming than others. It is up to the facilitator to decide when to move on.

Each session begins with Group Discussion. Take this time to relax and get to know one another, using the questions provided. These questions highlight the theme of the lesson, but feel free to ask your own. If your class is one hour, do not take more than ten minutes with these questions.

After the group discussion, begin your session with prayer. Invite the Holy Spirit to lead and guide you as you look into God's Holy Word. At the end of each lesson, you will find a Life Application. Encourage your group to put it into practice until you meet again. Finish each session with enough time for prayer.

How to do this Study on Your Own

Remember first that you are not alone! Begin and end your Bible study times in prayer, inviting the Holy Spirit to lead you as you look into God's Holy Word. Make use of the group discussion questions as they will aid you in your study. If something doesn't sit right with you or you disagree with anything in this study, that's okay! God promises us that His Word will not return to Him void (Isaiah 55:11). Remember, I am just a guide. Don't take my word for it; investigate for yourself. My desire in writing this book was to share with you what God showed me during times of Bible Study. It is my hope you will grow in your walk with the Lord and become a diligent student of the Word.

1. STANDING FIRM

It isn't easy being a follower of Christ. Our current culture is often intolerant of Judeo/Christian values and beliefs. Christians are becoming the minority in a world that has grown hostile towards us. This is why Daniel is the perfect book for today's Christian. Daniel and his friends Meshach, Shadrach, and Abed-Nego are excellent examples of godly men. They lived obedient and courageous lives for God. They did this while earning the admiration and respect of those who had taken them captive.

The book of Daniel was written for the Jewish people during their Babylonian captivity. The first half provides us with valuable lessons on how to live faith-filled lives. The second half of Daniel opens up a world that is both prophetic and historical in nature. I am sure it will encourage discussion and deep thought as you dig deeper into its truths.

Group Discussion:

Have you ever had to stand up for your faith? If so, what happened? How did it make you feel? What were the end results?

Read Daniel 1:1-21 and answer the following questions:

1. When do the events of this chapter occur?

2. Who was the king of Babylon and what did he do?

3. Read Daniel 1:2 and 2 Kings 24:14-15. Who did Nebuchadnezzar capture?

4. Read 2 Kings 24:14. Who was not captured by Nebuchadnezzar?

5. Read Daniel 1:2 and 2 Chronicles 36:18. What else did Nebuchadnezzar take from Jerusalem?

6. Where did Nebuchadnezzar take his captives?

The land of Shinar, also known as Babylonia, was the ancient name for Babylon. Babylon is in Iraq.

7. After Nebuchadnezzar took the vessels from the house of God, where did he put them?

If you are using an NIV or NASB, the Hebrew word for "official" is cariyc and it means "eunuch." Ashpenaz was the chief or master of the eunuchs.

8. The king ordered Ashpenaz to select youths from Israel and the royal family to serve in his court. What qualities did these youths require?

9. What did he order Ashpenaz to teach them?

10. How long were they educated?

11. What were the new names given to Daniel, Hananiah, Mishael, and Azariah?

12. What was Daniel determined not to do?

13. Who did Daniel seek permission from to carry out his plan?

14. What did Daniel propose to the chief of the eunuchs and what was the result?

15. What did God give Daniel, Hananiah, Mishael, and Azariah? And what was Daniel's particular gift?

16. What did the king find unique about them?

17. How long did Daniel serve the king?

This first chapter of Daniel shows us what God will do for those who wish to honour Him. Daniel did not want to defile himself with the king's food. As an Israelite, many foods were forbidden to him, foods that were part of Nebuchadnezzar's meal plan. But Daniel trusted that if he honoured God, the Lord would hear and answer his request, which He did.

As we continue with our study, we will discover that because he stood firm in his faith, Daniel was a man highly esteemed by God.

LIFE APPLICATION: Have you ever had to stand up for your faith? What about your convictions, those areas of your life where you stand firm, never crossing the line? If lying is wrong, but telling the truth could hurt someone, would you still persevere in your conviction not to lie? Today, try to be aware of those areas in your life where you may be failing and be a Daniel. Stand firm.

2. NEBUCHADNEZZAR'S DREAM

The second chapter of Daniel is a long one. So we will take this in chunks because we don't want to miss anything. Before you begin, read Daniel 2. One of the most unusual things about this chapter is how God used a pagan king's dream to elevate His servant. When the Jews were exiled to Babylon, many were no doubt thinking the worst, but God had a plan. The Lord sent His children into a pagan land riddled with idol worship. Now the king of that land was about to meet the one true God through Daniel.

Group Discussion:

Have you ever felt nudged by God to go out of your comfort zone? If so, did you obey? If not, what held you back?

Read Daniel 2:1-45 and answer the questions below:

1. When did Nebuchadnezzar have his dreams?

2. Nebuchadnezzar was so disturbed by his dreams he couldn't sleep. Who did he call to help him?

It's interesting to note the type of people King Nebuchadnezzar contacts to help him with his dreams.

Then the king gave the command to call the magicians, the astrologers, the sorcerers, and the Chaldeans to tell the king his dreams. So they came and stood before the king. — Daniel 2:2 NKJV

The chart below shows you how much Nebuchadnezzar relied on the occult and dark arts for wisdom.

Subject	Hebrew/ Aramaic Word	Definition
Magician	*Chartom*	Diviner, magician, astrologer, engraver, writer (in derivative sense as one possessed with occult knowledge) (Strong's H2748)
Astrologer	*'ashshaph*	Necromancer, conjurer, astrologer, enchanter, Exorcist (Strong's H825)
Sorcerer	*Kashaph*	To practice witchcraft or sorcery, use witchcraft, sorcerer, sorceress (participle) (Strong's H3784)
Chaldean	*Kasdiy*	The inhabitants of Chaldea, living on the lower Euphrates and Tigris; those persons considered the wisest in the land (by extension) (Strong's H3778)

3. The people Nebuchadnezzar relied on did not know God and were active in the occult. What is one stipulation he gives to them about interpreting his dream?

4. What will happen to them if they can't understand his dream?

5. What is the reward for interpreting his dream?

6. The Chaldeans told the king he was asking something impossible. How did the king respond?

7. The King sends out a decree to destroy all the wise men of Babylon. Who did that include?

8. Daniel asked the king to give him time so he might interpret the dream. What did Daniel do next and why?

9. How was the dream revealed to Daniel and what was his response?

10. After Daniel received his answer from the Lord, what did he tell Arioch?

11. What opportunity was Daniel given to share with the king?

12. Why did Daniel insist he did not receive the answer to the dream because he was the wisest in the land?

13. Ultimately, who did Daniel make sure received the glory?

When Daniel describes Nebuchadnezzar's dream, he uses the Aramaic word *tselem*, which means "image" or "idol." Our modern day Bible translations use the word "statue" or "image." But I want you to keep in mind the original intent of the image Daniel describes. It is, in Nebuchadnezzar's mind, an idol. This would be all he knew. He did not know the God of heaven. Yet God spoke to him in terms he would understand. Daniel begins by making sure Nebuchadnezzar knows his dream is from the one true God, and it is about the future.

> *"You, O king, were watching; and behold, a great image! This great image, whose splendor* was *excellent, stood before you; and its form* was *awesome."*—Daniel 2:31 NASB

The interesting thing to note here is the use of the word "awesome," which is found in the NASB and the NIV. It does not correspond to the actual meaning of the Aramaic word *děchal*, which, when translated, means "terrible" or "fearsome." To use the word *awesome* gives the modern day reader the sense that it was incredible to look at or "cool" when in fact Daniel was trying to convey that it was a fearful and terrible thing to see.

Modern words often mean something different when compared to the original Hebrew, Greek or Aramaic text. This is why literal translations of the Bible are not always the best to use alone. It is always good to have a Bible that is also "meaning-based." In other words, the meaning is determined by the context. Not all words should be taken literally. That would be unreliable because we know all words (no matter the language) have more than one meaning. They must be translated in accordance with the text surrounding them.

Using Daniel 2:31 as an example, let's do a word and translation search using the NIV and the KJV. The KJV tends to be a literal translation while the NIV is a meaning-based translation (keeping everything in context). I believe it is always best to have each type of translation available when doing a Bible study as it helps define the verse in question by bringing it more into focus. I also use *Strong's Concordance* as my reference guide. As an example of what I'm talking about, I have highlighted some of the words that are translated differently in the NIV and the KJV.

*"Thou, O king, sawest, and behold a great **image**. This **great** image, whose **brightness** was **excellent**, stood before thee; and the form thereof was **terrible**."* —Daniel 2:31 KJV, emphasis mine

*"Your Majesty looked, and there before you stood a large **statue**—an enormous, **dazzling statue, awesome** in appearance."* —Daniel 2:31 NIV, emphasis mine

Original Aramaic	Biblical Translation	Aramaic Meanings
Tselem	Image/statue	Idol or image
Rab	Great/enormous	Great, captain, chief
Ziyv	Brightness/dazzling	Brightness, countenance or splendour
Yattiyr	Excellent	Pre-eminent, surpassing, excellent, extreme, extraordinary
Děchal	Awesome	Terrible, terrifying, fear, to make afraid, dreadful

You can see how differently this verse reads when we try to replace the meaning of the word with a modern translation. This is why it is so important to also read the surrounding text. The statue Nebuchadnezzar saw wasn't something awesome to look at. It was an idol whose brightness was so extraordinary it was terrifying. This is why Nebuchadnezzar was alarmed by his dream. He'd never seen an idol like it before. He'd never seen an idol that terrified him.

14. Now that you know the intended meaning of the words, describe the image Nebuchadnezzar saw.

15. Where did the stone strike the image and what happened to it?

16. What was crushed together and what was the result?

17. Who represents the head of gold?

18. Who gave Nebuchadnezzar his power?

An inferior kingdom would arise after Nebuchadnezzar's, then another that would rule over all the Earth. History has shown who these kingdoms were. They are as follows:

- Babylonian Empire
- Medo-Persian Empire (more commonly referred to as the Persian Empire)
- Greek Empire
- Roman Empire

19. What is unique about the fourth kingdom?

[34]You watched while a stone was cut out without hands, which struck the image on its feet of iron and clay, and broke them in pieces. [35]Then the iron, the clay, the bronze, the silver, and the gold were crushed together, and became like chaff from the summer threshing floors; the wind carried them away so that no trace of them was found. And the stone that struck the image became a great mountain and filled the whole earth. — Daniel 2:34-35 NKJV

[44]In the time of those kings, the God of heaven will set up a kingdom that will never be destroyed, nor will it be left to another people. It will crush all those kingdoms and bring them to an end, but it will itself endure forever. [45]This is the meaning of the vision of the rock cut out of a mountain, but not by human hands—a rock that broke the iron, the bronze, the clay, the silver and the gold to pieces. — Daniel 2:44-45 NKJV

20. God will set up a kingdom that will never be destroyed. A stone represents it. Who is the stone?

21. What did Nebuchadnezzar say after Daniel interpreted his dream?

22. What did Nebuchadnezzar do after Daniel interpreted his dream?

23. What happened to Shadrach, Meshach, and Abed-Nego?

24. God was glorified through Nebuchadnezzar's dream because Daniel waited on the Lord and trusted Him to reveal all things. This is one of the hardest things for Christians to do: wait on the Lord. Can you think of a time when you waited on the Lord for direction or wisdom? What happened?

One of the most amazing things about the second chapter of Daniel is the revelation of Jesus Christ, our Rock and our Saviour, as the stone in the image. He alone will break the iron, clay, bronze, gold, and silver (kingdoms/countries) to pieces, to become like chaff. The most important of which is that no matter how much power today's presidents, kings, leaders, and rulers think they have, it will all be done away with when Christ returns.

LIFE APPLICATION: When Daniel heard a decree had been issued to slay all the wise men of Babylon, he boldly went before the king and asked for time to interpret his dream. He never waivered in his belief that God would answer him. Today, when you are praying, believe that God will answer and when He does, don't be afraid to act.

3. INTO THE FIERY FURNACE

God revealed Nebuchadnezzar's dream to Daniel and gave him understanding. What does Nebuchadnezzar do after he hears the correct interpretation of his dream? Does he look to the future and wonder about the other countries that will come to conquer him? No. Does he fortify his kingdom in preparation for the future? No. Does he fall down and worship God for making him (as Daniel calls him) "a king of kings"? No. He goes out and builds a gold statue, an idol, and makes everyone worship it.

Group Discussion:

Has life ever dropped you in a storm of trouble where one bad thing after another keeps happening to you? What have you discovered about yourself and your relationship with God during these times?

Read Daniel 3:1-30 and answer the following questions:

1. Nebuchadnezzar made an image/idol of gold. How high and wide was it? *(Note: Some versions use a cubit in their translations. A cubit is approximately 18 inches or .5 metres, roughly the length of a man's forearm).*

2. Where did he set up the idol?

3. Who did Nebuchadnezzar gather together for the dedication of his idol?

4. Do you think the idol/statue was of Nebuchadnezzar? Why or why not?

5. What were the people commanded to do when they heard the music?

6. What would happen to them if they didn't worship the idol?

7. Who didn't worship the statue?

Did you notice that it was the Chaldeans who accused the Jews? These were the same men Daniel rescued when they failed to interpret Nebuchadnezzar's dream. They lost lofty positions to Daniel, Shadrach, Meshach, and Abed-Nego. They were jealous, angry, and looking for a reason to get rid of Daniel and his friends. Daniel was the ruler over the entire province of Babylon. Nebuchadnezzar had placed him in charge of all his wise men. This would include the Chaldeans.

Moreover, at Daniel's request the king appointed Shadrach, Meshach and Abed-Nego administrators over the province of Babylon, while Daniel himself remained at the royal court. —Daniel 2:49 NKJV

8. Why do you suppose the Chaldeans did not include Daniel in their accusations?

9. Nebuchadnezzar, in rage and fury, ordered that Shadrach, Meshach, and Abed-Nego appear before him. What choice did he give them and how did the three men respond?

10. What happened to the men who threw Shadrach, Meshach, and Abed-Nego into the furnace?

11. What did Nebuchadnezzar see in the furnace?

12. Who did he liken the fourth person to?

13. When Shadrach, Meshach, and Abed-Nego came out of the furnace, what did everyone notice?

14. What did the king declare should be the case from that day on?

15. Examine your heart. You face the choice of a tortuous death or renouncing your faith. Which would you choose? Would you make your last breath count? Would you make it known that God is able to deliver you and if not, that you would be willing to die anyway?

LIFE APPLICATION: Their faith was tested and literally put to the fire. Shadrach, Meshach, and Abed-Nego trusted in God no matter what the outcome would be. They believed He could deliver them and if God chose not to, they would die for Him. Today, Christians in Muslim dominated countries and in communist countries face daily persecution, while those of us in the West have known little to no persecution. Pray for the persecuted church today.

4. GOD IS IN CONTROL

Nebuchadnezzar declared his belief in the God of Israel. Yet he still had some lessons to learn. Today we will look at how far God will go to reach those He loves.

Group Discussion:

Has God ever spoken to you in an unusual way? How did you know it was God? How did it change your life?

Read Daniel 4:1-37 and answer the following questions:

1. Who wrote this chapter?

2. Who was the chapter written to?

3. Why was it written?

4. Nebuchadnezzar has another dream. Who did he call first to interpret it and what does this suggest about him?

5. When Daniel finally stood before him, what did Nebuchadnezzar call him?

6. Who represented the tree in the dream?

7. What happened to the tree?

8. What does Daniel say will happen to the King?

9. Why is the King sent to live with the beasts of the field? What is the purpose behind it?

10. What advice does Daniel give the king?

11. When did all this happen to the king and what did he say before it happened?

There is nothing to suggest the king was thrown out of his kingdom by others. But everything suggests God caused him to go insane. Scripture says, *"While the word was still in the king's mouth, a voice fell from heaven: 'King Nebuchadnezzar, to you it is spoken: the kingdom has departed from you!'"* —Daniel 4:31 NKJV

And they shall drive you from men, and your dwelling shall be with the beasts of the field. They shall make you eat grass like oxen; and seven times shall pass over you, until you know that the Most High rules in the kingdom of men, and gives it to whomever He chooses. —Daniel 4:32 NKJV

Who are "they?" I'm inclined to believe it is the "watchers" or angels Nebuchadnezzar saw in his dream. God uses angels many times throughout the Bible to pronounce His judgments. I see no reason why He would not do so here.

12. How long was Nebuchadnezzar cast out of his kingdom?

13. Did Nebuchadnezzar ever come to his senses? If so, what happened?

Sometimes God has to bring us low before we look up. The next time you are going through a rough time, remember Nebuchadnezzar. He lost his sanity and his kingdom (for a time) so that he might recognize that God is King and is always in control.

LIFE APPLICATION: Today, ask God to show you if you are harbouring pride in your heart. If necessary, confess your sin and repent.

5. THE WRITING ON THE WALL

In Daniel 5 we suddenly have a new king. Though referred to as the *son* of Nebuchadnezzar, Babylonian cuneiform inscriptions suggest he was the eldest son of King Nabonidus, making Nebuchadnezzar his grandfather. However, there is also the belief that "son of" is a way of describing the succession of heirs to the throne.[1]

We are not told how much time has passed or how Nebuchadnezzar died, only that there is a new king in charge—but not for long.

Group Discussion:

Did you know that the phrase "the writing on the wall" is a suggestion of impending doom? Sometimes the signs are there that God is trying to get our attention. If we are sensitive enough to His Holy Spirit, we will see them. What do you do when you see "the writing on the wall?" Ignore it and hope for the best? Or acknowledge that God is trying to correct you and repent of your behaviour?

Read Daniel 5:1-31 and answer the following questions:

1. How many were present at Belshazzar's feast?

2. What did Belshazzar do to impress those in attendance?

3. Who did they praise?

Depending on the Bible version you use, Daniel 5:5 may be confusing. In the NIV, for example, the verse begins, *"Suddenly the fingers of a human hand appeared . . ."* But in the NKJV and the KJV, it reads, *"In the same hour the fingers of a man's hand appeared . . ."* It is important to note these differences because one translation assumes that things happened immediately after Belshazzar and his guests praised idols. The other implies it happened sometime during the hour. Strong's H8160 says the Aramaic word used was *sha'ah,* which means "a brief time, a moment, or in the twinkling of an eye." So, in this case, the NIV version is correct.

4. What was the king's response when he saw the hand appear?

5. Who did he call for and what did he promise them?

6.   The queen reminded the king about Daniel. What qualities about Daniel impressed her?

Did you notice the golden nugget of information the queen gives us about Daniel? She says in Daniel 5:11, "*. . . King Nebuchadnezzar your father—your father the king—made him* **chief** *of the magicians, astrologers, Chaldeans, and soothsayers"* (emphasis mine). This is incredible because it is the Magi (Chaldeans or Wiseman) from the East, who, centuries later, would go in search of the King of the Jews.

Have you ever wondered why these men who dabbled in the occult searched for the Jewish Messiah? It was because Daniel had been in charge of them. He would have instructed them in prophecy and told them what signs to look for in regards to the Messiah. This is a beautiful example of how God works to make His sovereignty known. Yes, God was punishing His people by exiling them to a foreign land. But at the same time, He was preparing their captors to be the ones who would search for the King of the Jews. God always has a plan and He is always several steps ahead of us, working things out for our good. Never forget that.

7.   Daniel reminds the king about what happened to his father, King Nebuchadnezzar, when pride overtook him. He then proceeds to tell the king that he is too prideful. What specifically does he say to him?

8. What was the warning written on the wall?

9. Who is Belshazzar's kingdom given to?

10. How did the king honour Daniel?

11. How and when did Belshazzar die?

Nebuchadnezzar's dream has come true. Another kingdom inferior to his has come into power. The Medo-Persian Empire now takes over the Babylonian Empire. This empire is one of the heads of the seven-headed beast in Revelation 13 and Daniel 7.

Both Nebuchadnezzar and Belshazzar had a problem with pride. Both worshipped idols. But did you notice what happened to them in the end? Nebuchadnezzar received mercy from God when he temporarily lost his mind. Why? Because, in the end, he humbled himself and recognized Yahweh as the true God.

Belshazzar did not receive mercy but died the night he saw the writing on the wall because he knew the story of his father (Daniel 5:22) yet refused to acknowledge the Lord as the true God. When pride overtakes us, the Lord will find a way to humble us and bring us back into a right relationship with Him.

LIFE APPLICATION: In the last lesson you asked God to show you where there was pride in your life. Today, acknowledge Him as your King and sit quietly at His feet. Don't ask for anything. Don't pray a list of concerns. Just listen.

6. THE LION'S DEN

Shadrach, Meshach, and Abed-Nego had their moment of testing in the fiery furnace. Now Daniel has his faith tested. It is interesting to note that so far, each king Daniel served had the power of God revealed to him. Each had to make a choice whether or not to believe in God. Yet, for the kings to believe, it was God's servants who suffered extreme tests of their faith. Sometimes we may wonder why we go through tough times or suffer persecution for our faith. It may be God is using us to reach another.

Group Discussion:

When you go through difficult times, how do you react? Do you rely on God more or your friends and family? Do your Bible study times suffer? What do you do to strengthen your relationship with God during hard times?

Read Daniel 6:1-28 and answer the following questions:

1. In Daniel 6:1, we run across the word "satrap" in the NASB, NIV, and NKJV. The KJV uses the word "princes." "Satrap" in Aramaic is 'achashdarpan and means "governor." How many governors (satraps) did Darius set over the kingdom?

In Daniel 6:2, we run into more confusion. The KJV uses the word "presidents" while the NKJV uses "governors." The NIV uses "administrators" and the NASB "commissioners." This can be confusing during a group Bible study if you aren't all using the same version of the Bible. Changing the Hebrew or Aramaic words into modern ones often misrepresents the original meaning. This is why it is helpful to have a *Strong's Concordance* on hand. In this case, the modern word "presidents" is appropriate because the Aramaic word used is *carek* and it means "chief or overseer."

2. How many presidents (overseers) were set over the governors (satraps)?

3. What was Daniel, a president or governor?

4. How did Daniel distinguish himself above the satraps and overseers?

5. What did the king think about doing for Daniel?

6. What did the satraps and overseers do in response to the king's decision?

The word "petition" is used in most translations of Daniel 6:7. In Aramaic, the word is *ba'uw*. In Jewish liturgy it means "prayer, petition or request."

7. What was done to trap Daniel and force the king's hand against him?

8. Did Daniel know what was done? What was his response?

9. How did the king react when he found out Daniel had disobeyed his edict? What did he try to do?

10. What did the king say to Daniel before he was thrown into the lion's den?

11. How did King Darius spend his evening while Daniel was in the lion's den?

12. The next day, how did the king show his belief that Daniel's God saved him?

13. How did the king retaliate against his satraps and overseers?

Daniel 6:7 says *all* the governors, administrators, satraps, counselors, and advisors consulted together. They wanted to trap Daniel and deceive the king. The Aramaic word used is *rĕgash*. It means "a tumultuous throng." It wasn't a few disgruntled men who approached the king. It was a large mob. All these men, as well as their wives and children, were thrown into the lion's den.

It is obvious the king was relieved Daniel had survived. He was also angry at the deception perpetrated upon him. Was it fair that the king punished the wives and children as well? Perhaps not. Yet the Scriptures are clear that it was done at the king's command. Regarded as property, wives and children had no rights during that time. So they were sent into the lion's den with their husbands.

"Men must tremble and fear before the God of Daniel." —Daniel 6:26

This proclamation by King Darius made it clear to all that Daniel's God was the living God. Because of this, Daniel prospered during Darius' reign and in Cyrus' reign as well.

When we have the opportunity to stand up for God and trust Him, He will honour that. We see this every day in the persecuted church. Believers in Christ face death because they refuse to agree to the demands of radical Muslims. Muslims are like the satraps and overseers in this lesson. They demand everyone worship no other god but Allah. Perhaps because of the way persecuted Christians are facing death today, some of these radical Muslims will come to Christ.

Here in North America, Christians aren't threatened with death for their faith. But there are still many ways we can be a witness of God's faithfulness. If you suffer from illness and there seems to be no let-up, don't let this defeat you. Remember Daniel and trust in God. He may be using your illness to reach another. Whatever your circumstances, always remember God is one step ahead of you in everything. He has already formed a plan. Trust Him and know He is able to do more than you can imagine. But don't forget your plans for your life may not be the same as God's. He may ask you to give your life for Him. If so, declare God's glory until your dying breath. God alone knows who will cross your path during your lifetime. He will use you in the best possible way to bring others to Himself. So don't lose faith. Just trust in God and know He is using you no matter where you are in life.

LIFE APPLICATION: We may never have to go through the ordeal of a blazing furnace or a den of lions, but life is not without its hardships. Today, if you are able and you know someone who is in need, reach out to them and ease their burden in some way. If you are the one who is laden down with troubles right now, don't keep them to yourself. Let someone else bring God's touch into your life today so that He may use them to help you.

7. STRANGE DREAMS

It is clear the book of Daniel is both prophetic and historical in nature. So to understand Daniel, we must put it in its historical context. Daniel tells us he had his dream in the first year Belshazzar was king of Babylon. This would be around 553 B.C. So this is before Belshazzar sees the writing on the wall. This reveals the book of Daniel is not in chronological order.

For the next little while, we will be spending some time in Daniel 7. We will be looking again at Daniel 2 and jumping ahead (just a little bit) to Daniel 8. We will also look at Revelation 12 and 13. All these chapters relate to one another even though they are different in nature, and you will see why in a moment.

For now, I want you to do something a little different. You will need several coloured pens or pencils. As mentioned in my preface, years ago I had training as a Precept teacher through Precept Ministries. The lessons I learned taught me how to study my Bible inductively, precept upon precept. We did this by marking up our Bibles—a lot. That is what I'm going to ask you to do. I want you to go through Daniel 7 and mark in blue every mention of Daniel's name, including pronouns. Also, I want you to mark every mention of God in purple and every mention of time in green. Why am I asking you to do this? Because it will help you learn more about Daniel, God, and the time period.

When you finish marking your Bible, go back and list what you have learned about Daniel and God. Then notice when these events took place. Write this information in your notebook or journal.

I'll get you started so you understand what I mean. Here is a little bit of what I learned about Daniel:

- He saw a dream and visions in bed. So it is possible he saw these things while asleep.
- He wrote his dream down and summarized it.
- He contemplated his vision.
- He grieved over what he saw.

Now do the same thing and see what you find out about Daniel, God, and the time or era these events happened. Do this before you answer the questions below.

Group Discussion:

Have you ever had a dream from God? How did you know it was God speaking to you? Note: I came to know the Lord through a dream. To learn more about it, visit www.laurajdavis.com/my-testimony.html.

Read Daniel 7:1-28 and answer the following questions:

1. What is the main event or subject of this chapter?

2. Where do the four great beasts come from?

3.   Describe the first beast and what happened to it.

We are now going to jump back and forth a bit in our Bibles. We want to see the connection between King Nebuchadnezzar's dream and Daniel's dream.

4.   Read Daniel 2:31-35 and describe the statue.

5.   Read Daniel 2:36-38. Who is the head of gold?

6.   Read Daniel 4:10-27. How is the tree in Nebuchadnezzar's dream like the first beast in Daniel 7:4?

7.   In Daniel 7:5 what did the second beast resemble? What was it doing?

8. What was the second beast commanded to do?

9. Read Daniel 2:32. What were the statue's breasts and arms made of?

10. Read Daniel 2:39. This second kingdom is also represented by the second beast. Was it as powerful a kingdom as Babylon?

11. Read Daniel 5:31. Who was the next ruler of Babylon after Belshazzar?

As you can see, both Daniel's and Nebuchadnezzar's dreams are related. Daniel 8:20 confirms this.

12. Read Daniel 7:6 and describe the third beast.

13. Read Daniel 2:32. What made up the belly and thighs of the statue?

14. Read Daniel 2:39. Where will the third kingdom rule?

15. Read Daniel 8:21. What is the name of the third kingdom, which is represented by the goat?

16. Read Daniel 7:7 and describe the fourth beast.

17. Read Daniel 2:33 and describe the legs and feet of the statue.

18. Read Daniel 2:40-43. What will the fourth kingdom do to all the other kingdoms?

19. Read Daniel 7:7. How was this kingdom different from all the others?

The fourth kingdom is a divided nation. We know from history it was the Roman Empire. In A.D. 330 Constantine founded the new capital of the Roman Empire. It existed on the site of the ancient Greek city Byzantium. Renamed Constantinople, it would become the capital of the Byzantine Empire. In A.D. 395 the Roman Empire divided in half. The Eastern Roman Empire was based in Constantinople, which is Istanbul, Turkey, today. The Western Roman Empire was located in Rome. Eventually, the Western Roman Empire fell. The Eastern Roman Empire survived and was called the Byzantine Empire.

We will end our lesson here. We have much to look at in regard to the ten horns that came out of the fourth beast. The next few lessons may seem like review to you, but it's good to reinforce what you know. So bear with me.

LIFE APPLICATION: Read a Bible commentary on who the four beasts were. It is always good to get other perspectives. You can find many commentaries online at www.Biblegateway.com.

8. THE ANCIENT OF DAYS

Before we look at the ten horns that came out of the fourth beast, let's consider the image Daniel presents of someone he calls "the Ancient of Days."

I kept looking until thrones were set up, and the Ancient of Days took His seat. His vesture was like white snow and the hair of His head like pure wool. His throne was ablaze with flames. Its wheels were a burning fire. A river of fire was flowing and coming out from before Him. Thousands upon thousands were attending Him, and myriads upon myriads were standing before Him. The court sat, and the books were opened. —Daniel 7:9-10 NASB

One of the things I do when jumping into a Bible study is to look at several different translations. More often than not, I will discover something that makes me dig deeper. Often I will notice how each interpretation differs from the other. For example, in the King James Version, the verse above begins, *"I beheld till the thrones were cast down . . ."* "Cast down" was the first phrase that jumped out at me and then I noticed the word "thrones" was plural, not singular. So then I had even more questions. But that is what—for me at least—makes Bible study interesting and fun. It forces me to look up the Hebrew, Aramaic or Greek words to find their proper definitions.

So what did the original Aramaic say? According to Strong's H7412, "cast down" is from the Aramaic word *rěmah*, which does mean "to throw or cast down" but also means "to put or place." So the above translation is a more modern way to say "thrones were set up." But why were thrones (plural) set up when only one was the primary focus? For that matter, who sat on the other thrones?

We find the answer when we compare scripture to scripture and this is when things get exciting. When we compare scripture to scripture, we discover why there was more than one throne and who was sitting on them.

Group Discussion:

What is the one thing you find most difficult about being a Christian? What is the one thing you find incredible about being a Christian?

Read the verses below and answer the following questions.

Read Revelation 4:1-10; Isaiah 6:1-3; Psalm 11:4; Psalm 93:1-2; Psalm 103:19; Ezekiel 1:25-27; and Daniel 7:9-10.

1.   Where does God's throne reside and what does God look like?

2.   Read Isaiah 6:1-3. Who was above God and what did they call out?

3. Read Revelation 4:3-5; Revelation 20:11; and Daniel 7:9-10. What does God's throne look like? Who surrounded God's throne?

4. Read Revelation 4:5. What noises came out of the throne?

5. Read Psalm 103:19. Who does God rule over?

What a spectacular scene! I think we can see that the Scriptures confirm the Ancient of Days is God. Now that you have a firm grasp on that, let's get back to the beasts.

Read Daniel 7:7-8 and answer the following questions:

6. How was the fourth beast different from all the others?

7. A little horn came up from the ten horns. What happened to three of the first horns?

8. How did this little horn act and speak?

9. Read Daniel 7:11-12. What happened to the fourth beast? What happened to the rest of the beasts? (Keep in mind that the beasts are kingdoms).

^{12} *(The other beasts had been stripped of their authority, but were allowed to live for a period of time.)* ^{13}*"In my vision at night I looked, and there before me was one like a son of man, coming with the clouds of heaven. He approached the Ancient of Days and was led into his presence.* ^{14}*He was given authority, glory and sovereign power; all nations and peoples of every language worshiped him. His dominion is an everlasting dominion that will not pass away, and his kingdom is one that will never be destroyed.—Daniel 7:12-14 NKJV*

10. According to the verses above, who was presented to the Ancient of Days?

11. What was given to the "Son of Man" and why?

12. How long will His dominion last? ("Dominion" in Aramaic is *sholtan* and also means "sovereignty" and "empire.")

13. What is unique about His kingdom?

14. Read Revelation 1:4-7. What has Jesus made us to be?

What an excellent reminder to us that God has dominion (sovereignty) over us and that we are His Kingdom! This is such a beautiful depiction of how much God loves us, that we are the kingdom, priests of God, whose righteous rule and authority over us is eternal. To think God loves us so much He chose us to be His kingdom is hard to get one's head around. It isn't *a place* that is the kingdom of God—*we* are the Kingdom of God. And His dominion over us will be everlasting.

Let that thought sink in and praise your heavenly Father for all He has done for you. We will look at the rest of Daniel 7 next time.

LIFE APPLICATION: You have been set aside by God to be His priest. You were chosen to serve in His kingdom. That kingdom is not far off into the future. That kingdom is now. Today, try to remember that as you interact with your family, friends, and strangers.

9. THE TEN HORNS

Before we get to the interpretation of Daniel's dream, I want to look at the ten horns that came up in Daniel 7:8-12. In our last lesson, you answered some questions about them. Today, we will go a little bit further toward discovering who they might be. There will not be any questions to answer today other than the group discussion question. Consider this a day of reflection on what you are about to read.

As we continue this study, we will notice parts of Daniel are historical prophecy. Other parts (like the ten horns) are still in our future. There are many different interpretations of who the ten horns could be. I will lay out for you the three most common theories that are around today and leave you to make your own decision.

Group Discussion:

What makes you believe we are living in the end-times?

The following are the various theories currently held in regard to the beast with the ten horns.

Theory Number One: The Roman Catholic Church

Many people believe the Roman Catholic Church (RCC) will play a role in fulfilling the prophecy of the beast with ten horns. Some prophecy teachers suggest the Antichrist will come in the form of the pope. In fact, for the past 500 years, Protestant church leaders have held that whoever holds the role of pope is the Antichrist. Luther himself believed the pope was the Antichrist when he said:

"This teaching shows forcefully that the Pope is the very Antichrist, who has exalted himself above, and opposed himself against Christ because he will not permit Christians to be saved without his power, which, nevertheless, is nothing, and is neither ordained nor commanded by God" (Martin Luther, Smalcald Articles, Part II Article IV: Of the Papacy).[2]

Great men of faith like Spurgeon, Wesley, Knox, Edwards, and others declared the Roman Catholic Church as the Whore of Babylon and the pope as the Antichrist.

The Westminster Confession of Faith of 1647 says, "There is no other head of the church but the Lord Jesus Christ. Nor can the pope of Rome in any sense be head thereof; but is that Antichrist, that man of sin and son of perdition that exalteth himself in the church against Christ and all that is called God."[3]

The great Methodist Preacher, John Wesley wrote this of the Catholic Church and the pope:

"He is in an emphatical sense, the Man of Sin, as he increases all manner of sin above measure. And he is, too, properly styled the Son of Perdition, as he has caused the death of numberless multitudes, both of his opposers and followers... He it is...that exalteth himself above all that is called God, or that is worshipped...claiming the highest power, and highest honour...claiming the prerogatives which belong to God alone." —Antichrist and His Ten Kingdoms, by John Wesley, pg. 110

From Luther to Bunyan, almost all great men of faith whom the Protestant church reveres have proclaimed the pope as the beast or Antichrist and the Roman Catholic Church as the Whore of Babylon. Scripture says the Whore of Babylon sits on seven hills (Revelation 17:9). Rome does sit on seven hills (or mountains) and the RCC does teach some doctrine that is contrary to the Bible. But how do they match up with the Scriptures? Is the coming beast another kingdom or a religion?

We know a false messiah is coming. Having a religion already in place that is prone to false doctrine is something Satan can use—especially if that same religion believes Muslims, Jews, and Christians all worship the same God. This would be beneficial for a deceiver who wanted to trick people into "worshipping the beast" (an ideology/religion or religious icon).

The great theologian R.C. Sproul says this about the Roman Catholic Church:

> "*At the moment the Roman Catholic Church condemned the biblical doctrine of justification by faith alone, she denied the Gospel and ceased to be a legitimate church, regardless of all the rest of her affirmations of Christian orthodoxy. To embrace her as an authentic church while she continues to repudiate the biblical doctrine of salvation is a fatal attribution.*"[A]

Clearly the RCC—and thus, the pope—are considered by some to be an apostate church, but do they qualify as "the beast"?

> [9] *Here is the mind which has wisdom. The seven heads are seven mountains on which the woman sits,* [10] *and they are seven kings; five have fallen, one is, the other has not yet come; and when he comes, he must remain a little while.* [11] *The beast which was and is not, is himself also an eighth and is one of the seven, and he goes to destruction.* [12] *The ten horns which you saw are ten kings who have not yet received a kingdom, but they receive authority as kings with the beast for one hour.* —Revelation 17:9-12 NASB

There is one thing people who promote the RCC theory have ignored: the seven hills are seven kings or kingdoms, not actual hills. Most believe it has to be the RCC because Rome sits on seven hills, but Jerusalem also sits on seven hills. However, I would not rule them out as having any influence in the world. The Vatican has the ear of the United Nations and has voting power. That's in addition to the estimated 1.2 billion people who are members of the Catholic Church. This could prove significant in how things will play out on the prophetic stage, particularly in regard to a one-world religion.

Theory Number Two: The European Union

It was once widely believed that the European Union, which formed after WWII, was the beginning of the ten kingdoms. The EU presently has twenty-eight countries/kingdoms in its membership. At its heart it is a type of government the Antichrist could easily step into, forming a one-world government. However, in recent months, England has talked of pulling out of the EU. If others follow her lead, we could find ten nations remaining. This could be the ten kings "who have not yet received a kingdom." Also, the symbol the EU uses (a woman riding on a beast) is startlingly prophetic.

". . . and I saw a woman sitting on a scarlet beast, full of blasphemous names, having seven heads and ten horns." —Revelation 17:3 NASB

A common interpretation of the above verse is that the woman symbolizes a *religious* Babylon and the beast symbolizes a *political or commercial* Babylon. If that is so, the RCC combined with the EU could be the stepping stone from which the Antichrist will emerge. The website www.seekingtruth.co.uk says this in regard to the RCC and the EU:

Revelation 17 describes the woman as "Babylon the Great" whilst Revelation 18 describes the fall of a commercial Babylon. In simplistic terms, a corrupt apostate church rides (and therefore by implication, controls) a corrupt and brutal political and commercial system.[5]

But do we see a religious Babylon in the E.U.?

The European Union flag has twelve gold stars on a blue background. Officially, it is claimed that the circle of twelve stars stand for "the ideals of unity, solidarity and harmony among the peoples of Europe. The number of stars has nothing to do with the number of member countries though the circle is a symbol of unity."[6]

Whenever we see a picture of Mary in the Catholic Church, she always has a halo of twelve stars around her head. This depiction comes from the Roman Catholic belief that Mary is the woman talked about in Revelation 12:1. Whereas, the Bible confirms that the woman is representative of Israel (Isaiah 54:1; 7-10; Micah 4:9-10; 5:3).

The UN recognizes the Vatican as a sovereign state. And the pope has full rights as head of state to address the UN General Assembly. Therefore, the Vatican can influence debate at the highest levels of government. They can effect change within the UN and the EU. Could we be looking at a one-world religion/government started by the EU and the RCC? Anything is possible.

Consider the current endeavours in Berlin by Christians, Jews, and Muslims to build the House of One. "This building will house a church, synagogue and Mosque all under the same roof, with a common room for inter-faith worship and dialogue at its centre."[7] This sets the stage for a one-world inter-faith government. But even knowing all this, how does it compare to the Scriptures?

[9] *Here is the mind which has wisdom. The seven heads are seven mountains on which the woman sits,* [10] *and they are seven kings; five have fallen, one is, the other has not yet come; and when he comes, he must remain a little while.* [11] *The beast which was and is not, is himself also an eighth and is one of the seven, and he goes to destruction.* [12] *The ten horns which you saw are ten kings who have not yet received a kingdom, but they receive authority as kings with the beast for one hour.* [13] *These have one purpose, and they give their power and authority to the beast.* —Revelation 17:9-13 NASB

Currently, the EU would have to reduce to ten member nations to qualify for this verse. Five of those nations would have had to have fallen at the time Revelation was written. Also, the beast would have to have been a part of the seven-headed beast. But it makes a good argument for verse thirteen, which says, "They have one purpose and they give their power and authority to the beast." A united RCC and EU could make worshipping the beast (who or whatever that will be) a reality.

Theory Number Three: Islamic Caliphate

For background, please read Revelation 13:1-18; Revelation 17:8-18; Daniel 2:31-45; Daniel 7:7-13.

You may have noticed that Nebuchadnezzar's statue and Daniel's vision of the beasts are similar to the beasts in Revelation 13 and 17. We know from previous study that the statue represented four kingdoms: Babylon, Persia, Greece, and Rome. But what I didn't point out was the ten horns in Daniel 7 and 13. They are represented by ten toes on Nebuchadnezzar's statue. Amazing, isn't it? That the Lord would give these two very different men dreams about the future? Especially when you read Daniel 2:34, which talks about the stone that struck the statue and became a great mountain that filled the whole earth. That stone was Jesus. And the mountain that filled the whole earth? His kingdom, which is indestructible. Daniel 7:18 adds further confirmation of this:

> But the saints of the Highest One will receive the kingdom and possess the kingdom forever, for all ages to come. —Daniel 7:18 NASB

Keep this in mind when thinking about the future. There is no need to fear because Jesus will fill the whole earth and the saints will receive the kingdom and possess it forever.

The following table will help you see more similarities between Nebuchadnezzar's statue, the beasts in Daniel's dream, and the beasts in Revelation.

Beasts of Revelation and Daniel

Revelation 13:1	This is one beast with ten horns, seven heads, and ten crowns on his heads who comes from the sea.
Daniel 7:3,7	These are four different beasts/kingdoms but the last one had ten horns.
Daniel 2:36-43	Nebuchadnezzar's statue represented four different kingdoms. There were ten toes on the feet of the statue similar to the ten horns of Revelation 13:1.
Revelation 13:2	The beast from the sea looked like a leopard, and his feet were like those of a bear, and his mouth like the mouth of a lion.
Revelation 13:11	The beast from the earth had two horns like a lamb but spoke like a dragon. He makes the earth and those who dwell in it worship the first beast.
Daniel 7:4-7 Daniel 2:31-35	The first beast was like a lion and had the wings of an eagle. Its wings were plucked, and it was lifted up from the ground and made to stand on two feet like a man. It was given a human mind. This represented Nebuchadnezzar and Babylon. The second beast resembled a bear. It was raised on one side and three ribs were in its mouth between its teeth. This represented King Cyrus and Persia. The third beast was like a leopard, but had four wings on its back. This beast also had four heads and dominion was given to it. This represented Alexander the Great and his four generals, which was Greece. The fourth beast was terrifying and extremely strong with large iron teeth. It devoured, crushed, and trampled the other beasts. It was different from all the other beasts as it had ten horns. It represented the Roman Emperors from Herod on down and ten future kingdoms.
Revelation 13:3	One of the heads died and was healed. The whole world followed after it.

Beasts of Revelation and Daniel

Daniel 7:8	A little horn came up among the ten horns and three of the first horns were pulled out by the roots before it and this horn possessed eyes like the eyes of a man and a mouth uttering great boasts.
Revelation 13:7	This "head" or king was also given the power to make war with the saints and overcome them. He was given authority over every tribe and people, tongue, and nation.
Daniel 7:25	This "horn" or king will speak out against the Most High and wear down the saints of the Highest One.
Revelation 17:9-13	The seven heads are seven mountains that are also seven kings. Five have fallen, one is, and the other has not yet come. When he comes, he must remain a little while. The beast that was and is not is himself also an eighth and is one of the seven. He goes to destruction. The ten horns are ten kings who have not yet received a kingdom, but they receive authority as kings with the beast for one hour. These have one purpose and they give their power and authority to the beast.
Daniel 2:44-45 Daniel 7:13-14 Daniel 7:18	God sets up a kingdom that will never be destroyed during the time of these kings. It will crush and put an end to all the nations, but it will itself endure forever. A stone cut out of the mountain without hands crushes the iron, bronze, clay, silver, and gold. The saints of the Most High will receive the kingdom and possess it forever.

You can see the similarities between the beasts in Revelation 13 and 17 and Daniel 2 and 7. Fortunately, Daniel's vision is explained for him, and because of that, we are given a glimpse of what the beasts in Revelation represent: kings and/or kingdoms.

We are also told in Revelation 17:9-10 that the seven heads of the beast of the sea represent seven mountains, which are also seven kings. Jeremiah 51:25 confirms that "mountains" refer to kingdoms. Revelation 13:3 tells us that one of these heads is mortally wounded and then healed, meaning one of the seven kingdoms died but will live again. In addition, Daniel 7:8 tells us about another horn that emerges from the ten horns and three of the first horns will be pulled up from the roots by it. This leaves us with a few questions:

- Which of the four kingdoms that has long been extinct has or will be revived to rule again?
- How did the four main kingdoms become seven kingdoms (seven heads)?
- How do the empires that reigned after Rome (Byzantine Empire, Ottoman Empire, etc.) factor in?
- Who is the little horn that emerges and who are the three horns that it uproots?
- Are we seeing the rise of any of these former empires today?

Scripture and historical fact reveal the four main kingdoms or beasts were:

- The Babylonian Empire
- The Medo-Persian Empire (more commonly referred to as the Persian Empire)
- The Greek Empire
- The Roman Empire

The Greek Empire was divided into four separate heads (or dynasties) as Daniel's dream foretold (Daniel 7:6). They were:

1. Egypt (Ptolemaic dynasty ruling from Alexandria—305B.C.)
2. Greece (Antogonid dynasty in Greece ruling from Macedonia—306B.C.)

3. Syria (Seleucid dynasty in Syria and Mesopotamia, which is modern day Iraq—305B.C.)
4. Asia Minor (Attalid dynasty in Pergamum—282B.C.; Asia Minor is Turkey)

This now gives us a clear picture of our seven-headed beast. The four main empires are highlighted.

1. **The Babylonian Empire (Nebuchadnezzar)**

2. **The Persian Empire (King Cyrus)**

3. **The Greek Empire (Alexander the Great).** Upon his death, his kingdom was divided into three separate kingdoms, making it into four kingdoms, which included Greece.
4. Egypt (Ptolemaic dynasty ruling from Alexandria)
5. Syria (Seleucid dynasty in Syria and Mesopotamia)
6. Asia Minor (Attalid dynasty in Pergamum—Turkey)
7. **The Roman Empire** (which absorbed all these empires into its own)

Which of the four kingdoms that have long been extinct has or will be revived to rule again?

> [23] *Thus he said: "The fourth beast will be a fourth kingdom on the earth, which will be different from all the other kingdoms and will devour the whole earth and tread it down and crush it.* [24] *As for the ten horns, out of this kingdom ten kings will arise; and another will arise after them, and he will be different from the previous ones and will subdue three kings."* —Daniel 7:23-24 NASB

We have established that the fourth beast was the Roman Empire, and we know from the former Roman Empire seven kings or kingdoms will emerge, five of which had already fallen at the time Revelation was given to John. We also know from

Revelation 17:9-12 that the beast once existed, now is not, and will come again. He is also part of the original seven. By the process of elimination, the following kingdoms had already fallen by the time John received Revelation:

- Babylonian Empire (Nebuchadnezzar)
- Persian Empire (King Cyrus)
- Greek Empire (Alexander the Great, Antogonid dynasty in Greece, ruling from Macedonia)
- Assyrian Empire (Seleucid dynasty in Syria and Mesopotamia, which was absorbed into the Roman Empire)
- Egyptian Empire (Ptolemaic dynasty ruled from Alexandria)

Who was the one that had not yet fallen at the time Revelation was written and would be the "one that is"?

- Roman Empire

Which kingdom "was and now is not" but is also an eighth king? Turkey (Asia Minor), a small country that grew into the Ottoman Empire.

I believe this for the following reasons:

- It no longer existed as an empire at the time John wrote Revelation.
- It remained for a short while.
- It belonged to the seven yet was an eighth king.
- History revealed the Babylonian, Persian, Greek, Egyptian, and Syrian empires never rose to be mighty empires again. In other words, they never rose again to conquer other kingdoms and take them over. Only one

former empire grew to become "an eighth": Asia Minor (Turkey), in the form of the Ottoman Empire.

The Turkish Empire, paved the way for a future Islamic Caliphate. I do not believe it is a revived Roman Empire headed by the Catholic Church that is coming. I believe it is a revived Ottoman Empire from the sub-kingdom of Turkey, which was absorbed into the Seleucid dynasty and finally into Rome itself.

"At its peak, the Ottoman Empire included Turkey, Egypt, Greece, Bulgaria, Romania, Hungary, Israel, Jordan, Lebanon, Syria, and parts of the Arabian Peninsula and North Africa."[8]

It does not qualify as the fourth kingdom because it never became as large as the Roman Empire, which stretched all the way from Africa to Britain and from Egypt to Syria (present-day Iraq). At the end of WWI, the Ottoman Empire was, like the Greek Empire, divided into several new states (or sub-kingdoms). The division brought about the creation of the modern Arab world we know today and the Republic of Turkey. The Ottoman Empire had revived the eighth beast in the form of Islam, its goal to create a Muslim Caliphate or Muslim State. Today, ten nations (or sub-kingdoms) surround Israel and they are:

- Turkey
- Syria
- Iraq
- Iran
- Saudi Arabia
- Egypt
- Jordan
- Sudan
- Libya
- Lebanon

Remember when I said in previous lessons that we need to compare scripture with scripture? Take a look at Psalm 83:1-8.

O God, do not remain silent; do not turn a deaf ear, do not stand aloof, O God. [2]See how your enemies growl, how your foes rear their heads. [3]With cunning they conspire against your people; they plot against those you cherish. [4]"Come," they say, "let us destroy them as a nation, so that Israel's name is remembered no more."

[5]With one mind they plot together; they form an alliance against you—[6]the tents of Edom and the Ishmaelites, of Moab and the Hagrites, [7]Byblos, Ammon and Amalek, Philistia, with the people of Tyre. [8]Even Assyria has joined them to reinforce Lot's descendants. —NIV

Today, almost all the names mentioned in the verse above comprise the modern Arab world, they all surround Israel, and they were all once a part of the Roman and Ottoman Empires.

With one mind they plot together; they form an alliance against you. — Psalm 83:5 NIV

Israel's enemies all hate her, they are all of one mind in how to destroy her, and they all surround her.

*"...Come," they say, "let us destroy them as a nation, so that Israel's name is remembered no more." —*Psalm 83:4 NIV

How many times have we heard leaders from Iraq, Iran, and other Arab countries say almost the same thing?

"After the Six Day War of 1967, one Arab leader after another has clearly stated that the only way of gaining peace in the Middle East is by the total annihilation of Israel as a nation. This remains the crux of the Arabic-Muslim position, in so much that most of the Arab nations refuse to recognize Israel's right to even exist."[9]

Could these ten Arab countries be the ten horns that represent ten kings/kingdoms? It's quite possible. It is no coincidence that they surround Israel today. But who might the little horn be, talked about in Daniel 7:8, from whom three horns were uprooted? This could still be in our future or it could be a terrorist group like ISIS, that is currently at war with the world, which includes several Muslim nations. This remains a mystery, but what we do know is that the stage is set and as we can see from the nightly news, we are getting closer and closer to Jesus' return.

LIFE APPLICATION: Take some time to evaluate what you have learned today. There are lots of theories out there, but they are just theories. Is it important that we know who the "end time players" will be? Not really. But it is important that we be prepared for them so we will not be deceived (Matthew 24:24). Spend some time in prayer and ask God to reveal His truths to you.

10. THE VISION INTERPRETED

Now we get to the interpretation of Daniel's dream. Aren't you glad God provided the explanation through an angel? Like King Nebuchadnezzar, Daniel also had a dream about the coming four kingdoms. A statue represented Nebuchadnezzar's dream. Four beasts symbolized Daniel's dream. Today we will look at the interpretation of the beasts and compare them to the beasts in Revelation.

Group Discussion:

Jesus commands us to pray for our enemies. Most people don't have personal enemies, but countries do and many of them are at war with Muslim extremists like ISIS. Do you pray for Muslim extremists? Why or why not?

Read Daniel 7:15-28 and answer the following questions:

1. Who do the four beasts represent?

2. Who will receive the kingdom and possess it forever?

3. How many horns are on the fourth beast's head?

4. Where do the ten horns come from (Daniel 7:24)?

5. Another king will arise, different from the others. How many kings does he subdue (Daniel 7:24)?

6. Who will he speak against and oppress? How will he do it (Daniel 7:25)?

Revelation 17:12-13 tells us a little more about the beast and what his heads represent. Read it now. The following table will show you the clues from the Bible that reveal who the kingdoms/beasts are. It starts back with King Nebuchadnezzar in Daniel 2. Read it again to get a better understanding. Then look at the following table.

The Four Kingdom Beasts

CLUES	VERSE	MEANING	KINGDOM
Head of gold; looked like a lion with plucked eagle's wings; it was made to stand like a man	Daniel 2:36-38; Daniel 4:34-36; Daniel 7:4; Rev.13:1-2	Nebuchadnezzar was a king of kings who boasted of his own glory. He went mad and had his kingdom	The first kingdom is Babylon. Nebuchadnezzar 626 B.C.

CLUES	VERSE	MEANING	KINGDOM
		taken, but it was restored to him.	
Chest and arms of silver; looked like a bear raised up on one side with three ribs in its mouth; feet like a bear; ram with two horns	Daniel 2:32-39; Daniel 7:5; Jeremiah 51:11; Isaiah 13:17-20; Daniel 6:28; Daniel 8:20; Revelation 13:2	Another inferior kingdom rose; it subdued the other kingdom; Darius the Mede was king over the Chaldeans, Cyrus was king over all	Medo-Persian Empire Darius the Mede/Cyrus the Great 539 B.C.
Belly and thighs of bronze; like a leopard with four wings on its back; had four heads and dominion was given to it.	Daniel 2:39; Daniel 7:6; Daniel 8:21-22; Daniel 11:2; Revelation 13:2	The third kingdom ruled over all the earth. There were four kingdoms (heads): Ptolemy who took Egypt, founded the Ptolemaic dynasty, ruled from Alexandria (305 B.C.); Antigonus established the Antogonid dynasty in Greece from Macedonia (306B.C.); Seleucus established the Seleucid dynasty in Syria and Mesopotamia (305B.C.); Philetaerus established the Attalid dynasty	Macedonian (Greek) Empire; Alexander the Great, the king of Macedonia, conquered all of Asia Minor (Turkey, which was the Persian Empire) in less than two years. Alexander's empire stretched from Egypt to India. After his death his kingdom was split four ways, with four of his generals taking control. 331 B.C.

CLUES	VERSE	MEANING	KINGDOM
		in Pergamum in Asia Minor (282B.C.)	
Legs of iron with feet of iron and clay; feet and toes partly of clay, partly of iron; dreadful, terrible, and exceedingly strong; different than all the other kingdoms before it; it had ten horns on its head that represent ten kings. One of these kings will subdue three of the other kings.	Daniel 2:40-44; Daniel 7:7; Daniel 7:20-27; Revelation 13:1; Revelation 17:9-14	The fourth kingdom is strong as iron. It will break into pieces and crush all others. The kingdom will be divided. It will be partly strong and partly fragile. In the days of the ten kings, God will set up a kingdom that will never be destroyed. It shall crush and consume all the other kingdoms. Jesus came during Roman rule. It is His kingdom that will never be destroyed.	Roman Empire conquered (Macedonian) Empire 168 B.C. Emperor Diocletian divided Rome in two (West and East in A.D. 284). In A.D. 476, the last Roman emperor in the west, Romulus Augustulus, was removed from power by Odovacar, leader of the Goths. This date is usually used by historians as the year the Roman Empire ended. However, Roman rule continued in the eastern empire for a number of years after this date — in modern Greece, Turkey, the Middle East, and northern Egypt.[10]

As you can see from the table above, the prophecies in Daniel and Revelation have been fulfilled up to the Roman Empire. Keep in mind that the first four beasts (kingdoms) are part of the seven-headed beast. So they are included here. We talked about this in the previous chapter, but I include it here again for review. The kingdoms are as follows (highlighted kingdoms are the original four beasts):

1. **The Babylonian Empire**

2. **The Persian Empire**

3. **The Greek Empire** (which broke off into three separate kingdoms, making it into four kingdoms, including Greece)
4. Egypt
5. Syria (Assyria)
6. Asia Minor (Turkey)
7. **The Roman Empire** (which absorbed all these empires into its own)

> [40] *Then there will be a fourth kingdom as strong as iron; inasmuch as iron crushes and shatters all things, so, like iron that breaks in pieces, it will crush and break all these in pieces.* [41] *In that you saw the feet and toes, partly of potter's clay and partly of iron, it will be a divided kingdom; but it will have in it the toughness of iron, inasmuch as you saw the iron mixed with common clay.* [42] *As the toes of the feet were partly of iron and partly of pottery, so some of the kingdom will be strong and part of it will be brittle.* [43] *And in that you saw the iron mixed with common clay, they will combine with one another in the seed of men; but they will not adhere to one another, even as iron does not combine with pottery.* —Daniel 2:40-43 NASB

History proves that Rome did become a divided kingdom. But notice the last verse. The people would be a mixture and would not remain united. We tend to think of the Roman Empire as being somewhere around Italy, centred in Rome. But that was not the case. The Roman Empire, though divided, was vast and stretched from Britain to Asia Minor (Turkey).

The people were indeed a mixture of several different languages, cultures, and beliefs. They included people from present day countries like Great Britain, Germany, France, Italy, Scandinavia, Armenia, Spain, the Middle East, and of course, Turkey (just to name a few). And it was this last group the Roman Empire underestimated. It was the Turkish Muslims headed by the sultanate of the Osmanli/Ottoman dynasty that helped the Ottoman Empire grow in strength. The *beast who once was* (Turkey) and *now is not* (at the time of John's writing of Revelation) *was an eighth king*. That eighth king, as I stated before, was the Ottoman Empire. It was governed according to Islamic law, which relegated non-Muslims to second class status by denying them basic civil rights and requiring them to pay extra taxes. In fact, the Armenian massacres (up to 95 percent of Armenia is Christian) conducted from 1895 to 1922 were still going on during WWI. Today, the eighth beast continues its persecution towards Christians and Jews—and anyone else who will not bow to Allah.

[24] As for the ten horns, out of this kingdom ten kings will arise; and another will arise after them, and he will be different from the previous ones and will subdue three kings. [25] He will speak out against the Most High and wear down the saints of the Highest One, and he will intend to make alterations in times and in law; and they will be given into his hand for a time, times, and half a time. —Daniel 7:24-25 NASB

It is clear that the heads, crowns, horns, and hills all represent kings or kingdoms/dynasties. More importantly, the ten kings will come from the former Roman Empire. After these ten kings, another king will arise. He will subdue three of the ten kings and speak against God and oppress His holy people by trying to change the times and laws. I can think of only one religion today whose people are actively trying to change the laws to suit them. That religion is Islam and the law of the land they want everyone to follow is Sharia Law.

7. How long are the holy people delivered into the hands of the king who speaks against God (Daniel 7:25)?

8. What happens to this insolent king (Daniel 7:26)?

9. Who is given all the kingdoms under the whole of heaven?

10. How long will this kingdom last?

It is easy to become distraught and anxious these days when every news report we hear begins with another terrorist act by Muslim extremists. But keep your eyes focused on Jesus, the author and finisher of our faith. He is coming again to establish His kingdom, which shall be an everlasting kingdom and no one will be able to come against Him.

LIFE APPLICATION: With each new beheading by ISIS, we grow angrier and find it difficult to pray for our enemies. Yet Jesus commands us to pray for them. So today, pray for the members of ISIS, Boko Haram, Al 'Qaeda, etc., that the persecution and murders of our fellow brothers and sisters in Christ would have an impact on them and that many would turn to Christ because of the witness of these martyrs.

11. THE RAM AND THE GOAT

Today, we are going to break down Daniel 8, but to do that, it is important you read the entire chapter first. You will notice we are dealing with a totally different dream. Whereas Daniel 7 dealt with something that takes us into our future, Daniel 8 deals with our past. On a side note, if you are interested in seeing the ancient sites that Daniel mentions in this chapter, visit www.openBible.info/geo/. They are currently trying to make a "Google Map" of biblical places. It is a work in progress. Not everything is available, but it is very interesting and greatly enhances your Bible study times.

Group Discussion:

From here until the end of Daniel, we will be dealing with prophecies concerning the Jewish people and their history. What do you hope you will discover or take away from the rest of this study?

Read Daniel 8:1-27 and answer the following questions:

1. When did Daniel have his vision?

2. How many years had passed between Daniel's visions?

3. Where did Daniel see himself in the vision?

It is interesting to note that Daniel gives such detailed information as to his location. He says he was in the citadel (palace) of Susa, which is in the province of Elam. He then says he saw himself beside the Ulai Canal (river). If you look at a map, you will see the remains of the palace of Susa are far away from the Ulai River, which is still around today. Both of these locations are in modern day Iran.

4. What was standing beside the river?

5. How many horns did it have?

If you are using a King James Bible, you will notice Daniel 8:3 states the horns were high. Whereas the NASB, NIV, and other translations say the horns were long. The original word in Hebrew is *gaboahh* and it does not mean "long." It means "high or higher." It also means (and this is important) "proud, lofty, and haughty." Keep this in mind as we look at these horns.

6. Where was the ram pushing?

Read Daniel 8:20-22 and answer the following questions:

7. Who was the ram?

8. Who was the male goat?

9. What did the goat have between his eyes and what did it represent?

In Daniel 8:5, most translations say the male goat came across the earth "without touching the ground." This may sound like the goat was flying, which would be very strange indeed. But we have the advantage of history. We know the male goat represents the kingdom of Greece (Daniel 8:21). The Greek Empire grew fast and was one of the largest empires of the ancient world. It stretched from Greece to Egypt and into northwest ancient India. Alexander the Great was the head of the Greek Empire. Undefeated in battle, he was one of history's most successful military commanders. So Daniel saw the Greek Empire spread far and wide, ultimately conquering the Persian kingdom.

10. What did the goat do to the ram (Daniel 8:5-8)?

11. What happened when the large horn on the goat was broken?

Skipping down to Daniel 8:20, we have confirmation that the two-horned ram represents the kings of Media (Darius) and Persia (Cyrus the Great). The shaggy goat is the kingdom of Greece and the large horn between its eyes is the first king (Alexander the Great).

Notice what verses 8-9 say:

[8]*Then the male goat magnified himself exceedingly. But as soon as he was mighty, the large horn was broken; and in its place there came up four conspicuous horns toward the four winds of heaven.*[9]*Out of one of them came forth a rather small horn which grew exceedingly great toward the south, toward the east, and toward the Beautiful Land.* —NASB

Verse 8 tells us the Greek Empire became very great, but at the height of its power, the large horn (Alexander the Great) was broken off (died) and in its place four prominent horns

(Egypt, Greece, Syria, and Asia Minor [Turkey]) grew up. Verse 9 then gives a very important clue. One of these four dynasties would grow in power to the south, east, and toward "the beautiful land," which is Israel. So we need to look at history again to see which one it was and we will talk about the little horn that grew and its implications in our next lesson.

LIFE APPLICATION: God always has a plan. As we go through the rest of this study, you will begin to see the Scriptures come to life as history plays itself out in its pages. So today, look back on your life and make a list of significant life events (those "God moments") that impacted you. For example, when I look back on my life, I see God's hand everywhere, even before I acknowledged Him as my Saviour. He revealed His power and His might to me when I was eight years old by answering a prayer I offered while in the middle of a tornado. Yet I didn't commit my life to Him until I was seventeen. But it had such a huge impact on me that it started my journey toward God. What significant life events turned you toward the Lord? When you look back on your life, where do you see His hand?

12. THE BIG REVEAL

Today, we will look at the horns and the interpretation of Daniel's dream. As discussed in the previous lesson, the male goat represented the Greek kingdom, and at the height of its power the large horn, which represented Alexander the Great, was broken. History confirms that at the height of his power, Alexander the Great died.[11]

It grew up to the host of heaven and caused some of the host and some of the stars to fall to the earth, and it trampled them down. —Daniel 8:10 NASB

His power will be mighty, but not by his own power, and he will destroy to an extraordinary degree and prosper and perform his will. He will destroy mighty men and the holy people. —Daniel 8:24 NASB

Group Discussion:

What should the church be doing in preparation for Jesus' return?

Read Daniel 8:9-27 and answer the following questions:

1. Daniel 8:24 interprets Daniel 8:10. The stars were not angels or actual stars. Who were they?

2. Out of the four horns, a small horn grew exceedingly great. In other words, one general had a small dynasty that grew larger. How big was his dynasty? Where does scripture say it stretched to (Daniel 8:9)?

3. According to Daniel 8:14, how long would the Temple be desolate and the sacrifices cease?

4. Who helped Daniel understand the vision (see vs.16)?

5. Who did the ram with two horns represent (Daniel 8:20)?

6. Who was the shaggy goat? And who did his large horn represent?

7. From which nation will the four kingdoms (four horns) come?

8. In the latter part of the four kingdoms' rule, a king will arise. This man will be "shrewd and cause deceit by his influence, will magnify himself in his heart and destroy many while they are at ease." Who else will he oppose (Daniel 8:25)?

9. How will he be stopped?

10. What was Daniel ordered to do after he received the vision?

Now that you have searched the Scriptures for truth, let us see where this is in history.

⁸Then the male goat magnified himself exceedingly. But as soon as he was mighty, the large horn was broken; and in its place there came up four conspicuous horns toward the four winds of heaven.

[9]Out of one of them came forth a rather small horn which grew exceedingly great toward the south, toward the east, and toward the Beautiful Land.
—Daniel 8:8-9 NASB

So who were these four horns? After Alexander the Great died, his kingdom was divided into four separate dynasties, or kingdoms, between four of his generals. They were once again:

1. Egypt (Ptolemaic dynasty rules from Alexandria—305 B.C.)
2. Greece (Antogonid dynasty in Greece ruling from Macedonia—306 B.C.)
3. Syria (Seleucid dynasty in Syria and Mesopotamia, which is modern day Iraq—305 B.C.)
4. Asia Minor (Attalid dynasty in Pergamum, in Asia Minor—282 B.C., Asia Minor is Turkey)

Daniel 9:27 had a very cryptic message about one of those generals that would be discussed by Jesus Himself as a warning to those living in the end times (Matthew 24:15).

And he shall confirm the covenant with many for one week: and in the midst of the week he shall cause the sacrifice and the oblation to cease, and for the overspreading of abominations he shall make it desolate, even until the consummation, and that determined shall be poured upon the desolate. — Daniel 9:27 KJV

The word "week" in Hebrew is *shabuwa`* and can mean seven days or seven years. The general consensus among scholars is that the one week mentioned in Daniel 9:27 refers to seven years. Some end times teachers believe this verse is talking about a future Antichrist. Most, however, acknowledge that Daniel 9:27 was about Antiochus Epiphanes IV. In spite of this, they still hold firm to the belief that a future Antichrist is coming who will be exactly like Antiochus.

The ruler of the Syrian kingdom (the Seleucid Dynasty), Antiochus Epiphanes IV, saw himself as a supreme god, meaning that he saw himself as having power over all the religions in his realm. He tried to change the traditions of the Jews and invented all manner of Greek beliefs to debase and humiliate them. For example, he built a gymnasium in Jerusalem and forced the priests to engage in "wrestling contests in the Greek fashion, which meant they were naked."[12] While some Greek Jews became Hellenized and willingly gave up their beliefs, those faithful to God were repulsed by this behaviour and it would lead to the Maccabean revolt. (More on that later.)

Antiochus also tried to alter the Hebrew Scriptures by introducing Greek beliefs into them. If anyone was caught reading the Torah, they were punished, sometimes even killed. Sabbath observation was abolished and circumcision was banned on pain of death. Jewish historian Josephus Flavius' account describes this as follows:

". . . Now Antiochus was not satisfied either with his unexpected taking the city, or with its pillage, or with the great slaughter he had made there; but being overcome with his violent passions, and remembering what he had suffered during the siege, he compelled the Jews to dissolve the laws of their country, and to keep their infants uncircumcised, and to sacrifice swine's flesh upon the altar; against which they all opposed themselves, and the most approved among them were put to death. Bacchides also, who was sent to keep the fortresses, having these wicked commands, joined to his own natural barbarity, indulged all sorts of the extremist wickedness, and tormented the worthiest of the inhabitants, man by man, and threatened their city every day with open destruction, till at length he provoked the poor sufferers by the extremity of his wicked doings to avenge themselves." —War, 1: 2; Whiston, V3: 11

In 167 B.C. Antiochus marched into Jerusalem, slew the high priest, dedicated the Temple to Zeus, erected an image of Zeus (in his own likeness) on the altar, desecrated the altar with pig's blood, and proclaimed himself God.[13]

[15]Therefore when you see the ABOMINATION OF DESOLATION which was spoken of through Daniel the prophet, standing in the holy place (let the reader understand), [16]then those who are in Judea must flee to the mountains.—Matthew 24:15-16 NASB

Those verses were a warning from Jesus, written by the Apostle Matthew. You will notice that Matthew inserted the words, "Let the reader understand." He did this because, at that point in time, the Maccabees' revolt had already taken place. Antiochus had tried to set himself up as God in the Temple and had desecrated it. He had already brought the sacrifices to an end. Therefore, Matthew and everyone in the early church knew, when Jesus said those words, He was referring to Antiochus and was warning them that it would happen again.

So did it happen again? Or are we still waiting for it?

Previous to its destruction in A.D. 70, General Pompey did go into the Temple in A.D. 63, thereby desecrating it, but he did not proclaim himself God. He did not remove anything and he did not stop the sacrifices. In fact, the next day he ordered the Temple cleansed and its rituals resumed.[14] However, the Jews continued to resist Roman occupation and in A.D. 70, just as Jesus predicted, the Temple was looted and burned to the ground. According to Josephus Flavius, the Roman soldiers grew furious with Jewish attacks, and against Emperor Titus' orders, set fire to the Temple. Thousands upon thousands of Jews, who, at that time were being slaughtered by the Romans, should have been fleeing Jerusalem to save their lives (in fact, Jesus had warned them to flee in Matthew 24:15-22). Instead, when they saw the Temple go up in flames, they ran back toward it to try to save it. Josephus shared the following:

". . . the rebels shortly after attacked the Romans again, and a clash followed between the guards of the sanctuary and the troops who were putting out the fire inside the inner court; the latter routed the Jews and followed in hot pursuit right up to the Temple itself. Then one of the soldiers,

without awaiting any orders and with no dread of so momentous a deed, but urged on by some supernatural force, snatched a blazing piece of wood and, climbing on another soldier's back, hurled the flaming brand through a low golden window that gave access, on the north side, to the rooms that surrounded the sanctuary. As the flames shot up, the Jews let out a shout of dismay that matched the tragedy; they flocked to the rescue, with no thought of sparing their lives or husbanding their strength; for the sacred structure that they had constantly guarded with such devotion was vanishing before their very eyes.[15]

The fury of the Roman soldiers was so great that anyone in their way, be they old men, women or children, were butchered on the spot. This was how the Temple fell the second time in A.D. 70. This was the abomination of desolation. The sacrifices stopped because the Temple was gone, and to this day, they have not been reinstated.

Here we must ask several questions because the answers will determine if the abomination of desolation will occur again in the future. We must find out the following:

a) Did Jesus consider the destruction of the Temple an abomination of desolation or were the Roman soldiers the atrocity? In other words, would any Gentile setting foot on the sacred ground of the Holy Temple be considered repugnant? Is the Dome of the Rock, for example, an abomination of desolation?

b) During Antiochus' reign, did he confirm a covenant for one week (seven years) with the Jewish people?

c) Has vision and prophecy been sealed up?

d) Was a decree issued to rebuild the Temple? If so, when was it issued and the Temple rebuilt?

e) Are the "people of the prince who is to come" in our past or our future?

f) Is the king that subdues three of the ten horns in Daniel 7:24 a future Antichrist who will have all the attributes of Antiochus?

We will look at these subjects and so much more in the lessons ahead.

LIFE APPLICATION: Jesus warned his disciples that another *like* Antiochus Epiphanes was coming again. Already we can sense a change in the world toward Christians that is hostile. This can cause some Christians great anxiety if they are not grounded in the truth. Today, reflect on the following verses and memorize your favourites: Isaiah 41:10; Philippians 4:6-7; Psalm 56:3; Deuteronomy 31:6; 1 Peter 5:6-7; Joshua 1:9; John 14:27. Satan often uses anxiety and fear to attack a Christian's sense of peace in God. Use these verses to repel those attacks.

13. SEVENTY WEEKS

From here on out, we may be jumping all over the place, but I will try to keep us on track. Many of the prophecies of Daniel 8 have to be looked at in connection with the prophecies of Daniel 9 and Daniel 11. In particular, Daniel 9:24-27, which says:

> ²⁴ *"Seventy weeks have been decreed for your people and your holy city, to finish the transgression, to make an end of sin, to make atonement for iniquity, to bring in everlasting righteousness, to seal up vision and prophecy and to anoint the most holy place.* ²⁵*So you are to know and discern that from the issuing of a decree to restore and rebuild Jerusalem until Messiah the Prince there will be seven weeks and sixty-two weeks; it will be built again, with plaza and moat, even in times of distress.* ²⁶*Then after the sixty-two weeks the Messiah will be cut off and have nothing and the people of the prince who is to come will destroy the city and the sanctuary. And its end will come with a flood; even to the end there will be war; desolations are determined.* ²⁷*And he will make a firm covenant with the many for one week, but in the middle of the week he will put a stop to sacrifice and grain offering; and on the wing of abominations will come one who makes desolate, even until a complete destruction, one that is decreed, is poured out on the one who makes desolate."*—Daniel 9:24-27 NASB

"Seventy weeks have been decreed ... to finish the transgression ..." That is seventy "sevens" or "years," which equals 490 years. This is not to be confused with the 70 years the Hebrews spent in exile in Babylon. Daniel learned about that prophecy through the prophet Jeremiah and realized then why they were in exile and how long it would last. To find out why the Jews were in exile, read Leviticus 25:3-7.

> *"For thus says the Lord, 'When seventy **years** have been completed for Babylon, I will visit you and fulfill My good word to you, to bring you back to this place.'"*—Jeremiah 29:10 NASB emphasis mine

Notice that it says years, not weeks. The Hebrew word used for years is *shaneh* and means "year" or "division of time." Whereas "weeks" (*shabuwa'*) can mean days or years.

Group Discussion:

First Peter 1:14-16 calls Christians to be holy. What does holiness mean to you and how do you practice it?

Read Daniel 9:1-19 and answer the following questions:

1. When does this chapter take place? Who was king?

2. What did Daniel observe?

3. How many years were set for Jerusalem to be left desolate?

4. How did Daniel react when he found out why God had sent the Jews into exile for seventy years?

5.   What did Daniel confess to God on behalf of his people?

If you haven't already done so, now would be a good time to invest in a *Strong's Concordance* and a Greek/Hebrew lexicon for doing word studies. Why? At some point in time, you are going to be reading your Bible in a group study and someone will notice a different word used, a word or two missing, or even extra words. This will lead to every member of your growth group wondering, "Which is the best translation?" For example, let's look at Daniel 9:24 in the KJV and compare it to the NASB. I will highlight missing words and added ones:

*"Seventy weeks are determined upon thy people and upon thy holy city, to finish the transgression, and to make an end of sins, and to make reconciliation for iniquity, and to bring in everlasting righteousness, and to seal up **the** vision and prophecy, and to anoint **the** most Holy."*—Daniel 9:24 KJV emphasis mine

*"Seventy weeks have been decreed for your people and your holy city, to finish the transgression, to make an end of sin, to make atonement for iniquity, to bring in everlasting righteousness, to seal up vision and prophecy and to anoint the most holy **place**."*—Daniel 9:24 NASB emphasis mine

First, let's look at the end of the verse and the omission of the word place from the KJV. Many translations add the word at the end, which leads one to believe that once again, the Temple or Holy of Holies will be anointed at some point in our future, leading many to believe the Temple will be rebuilt. However, after checking a copy of the Torah, I noticed it too left out the word place. This made me wonder why and begged the question: why is it included in some translations but not in others?

A proper word search revealed the word "holy" in Hebrew is *qodesh* and means "apartness, holiness, sacredness, separateness," something that is of God, a place, or even a thing (like a holy or sacred object in the Temple). The importance here is that it is anointed to signify its holiness. The NASB added the word place, while the KJV left it out, but they both included the phrase "the most holy" and that is significant. Why? Because in the original Hebrew text, "the most" also means *qodesh*. So it read *qodesh qodesh* or in English, "Holy of Holies" or "the most holy." In other words, that which is most holy will be anointed. So if you ever see something that looks inconsistent, try doing a word search with a *Strong's Concordance* and a Greek/Hebrew lexicon, as it can help put things in perspective for you.

Moving on . . . What does God's decree in Daniel 9:24 reveal? Let's get the Jewish perspective here. The Torah says in the JPS 1917 edition:

> *Seventy weeks are decreed upon thy people and upon thy holy city, to finish the transgression, and to make an end of sin, and to forgive iniquity, and to bring in everlasting righteousness, and to seal vision and prophet, and to anoint the most holy place.* —Daniel 9:24, JPS

Seventy weeks are decreed. Seventy weeks equals seventy sevens or years, which comes to 490 years. Now let's break this down. God's decree will:

- Finish the transgression (*pesha'*—meaning the Jews rebellion against God).
- Make an end of sin (Strong's GH2403 suggests the word "sin" can also be translated as "sin offering." When the Temple was rebuilt, the sin offerings were reinstated, making "an end of sin" for the Jewish people).

- Forgive iniquity. You may have noticed the original Hebrew does not include the words added in the KJV: "to make reconciliation." The Hebrew word for reconciliation is *kaphar* and it means "atonement." These words are not found in the Torah. It simply says "forgive iniquity." Iniquity means "premeditated choice, continuing without repentance," like King David's choice to sin with Bathsheba, which eventually led to the death of her husband (2 Samuel 11:3-4 and 2 Samuel 12:9). So, in this case, God will forgive their iniquity or premeditated sin. He is not asking them to make atonement for it.
- Bring in everlasting righteousness. Jewish thought is that only Temple worship can bring in everlasting righteousness, while Christians believe this is fulfilled through Jesus.
- Seal up vision and prophet (meaning Daniel's vision about this prophecy alone is sealed up).
- Anoint the most holy place (this would be in reference to the Holy of Holies).

So you are to know and discern that from the issuing of a decree to restore and rebuild Jerusalem until Messiah the Prince there will be seven weeks and sixty-two weeks; it will be built again, with plaza and moat, even in times of distress. —Daniel 9:25 NASB

From the time a decree is issued to restore and rebuild Jerusalem until Messiah the Prince, there will be seven weeks and sixty-two weeks, 483 years. But Daniel 9:24 says there will be seventy weeks (490 years). So why is there a seven-year gap?

Christians assert it is during this seven-year gap that the Antichrist will come and make a covenant of peace with Israel. Halfway through that seven year period the Antichrist will break his covenant and then Jesus will return. But is this interpretation correct?

In 169 B.C., Antiochus Epiphanes IV began his march on Jerusalem. During this time he implemented the changes to

Temple worship and laws I talked about previously. When he desecrated the Temple in 167 B.C., a priest by the name of Mattathias rose up against him with his five sons: John (also called Gaddi), Simon (also called Thassi), Judah (also called Maccabeus), Eleazar (also called Avaran), and Jonathan (also called Apphus). When Mattathias died in 166 B.C., his sons continued the fight against Antiochus and the Maccabean revolt began.

The date when Antiochus defiled the Temple was the 15th of Kislev (December) in 167 B.C. It was then that the sacrifices stopped. Three and a half years later, it was officially cleansed on the 25th of Kislev, 164 B.C. and the sacrifices resumed once more. This is why Hanukkah is celebrated annually by the Jews, for their Temple was cleansed and restored once more.

What is Hanukkah?

"The kindling of a seven-branched Menorah was an important component of the daily service in the Holy Temple. When the Maccabees liberated the Temple from the hands of Antiochus, they found only a small bit of pure and undefiled olive oil fit for fueling the Menorah. The problem was, it was sufficient to light the Menorah only for one day, and it would take eight days to produce new pure oil. Miraculously, the oil burned for eight days and nights and Hanukkah or Chanukah was born."[16]

He said to me, "For 2,300 evenings and mornings; then the holy place will be properly restored."—Daniel 8:14 NASB

Imagine a day that begins in the evening *and* in the morning. It seems crazy, doesn't it? And yet, for the Jews, the beginning of their day starts when the stars begin to appear and their morning begins with the appearance of the North Star. It is based on this verse in Genesis 1:5: *"God called the light day, and the darkness He called night. And there was evening and there was morning, one day."*

Therefore, when we are looking at 2,300 evenings and mornings, we are really looking at half that amount according to

Jewish time—1,150 days. One thousand and fifty days equals about three and a half years, the exact amount of time it took from the time Antiochus defiled the Temple until it was cleansed. Keep that in mind as we go forward.

LIFE APPLICATION: Take some time to read the rest of Daniel's prayer (Daniel 9:7-19) and think about the situation in your own country, city, province, or state. In Canada, where I live, I feel it is just a matter of time before God removes His protective hand from our country. We have thrown God out of our schools and even our government. Our new prime minister is actively campaigning for the murder of babies (abortion) and also wants to bring in assisted suicide laws. His disrespect for life will be detrimental to Canada's survival. In addition, our national anthem was deemed illegal by one city council in Ontario because of the words "God keep our land glorious and free."[17] Respect and honour for our holy God has all but vanished in Canada's government.

What laws are allowed in your country, province/state, or cities that dishonour God? What kind of rebellion exists towards God in your country? Today, take time to pray Daniel's prayer for your country, for all levels of government and for the inhabitants of the land.

14. WHO ISSUED THE DECREE?

Daniel has just prayed a heartfelt prayer to the Lord after he discovered the reason the people of Israel were in exile in Babylon (Leviticus 23:3-5). It was because they had sinned against God and had forsaken His laws and commandments that God punished them for their iniquity. For seventy years they would be in exile, in accordance with the amount of time the Israelites had not obeyed God's law about letting the land lie fallow during the seventh year. Now Daniel has discovered their sin and confessed it to God and the Lord is so moved by Daniel's prayer that He calls him "highly esteemed" (Daniel 9:23) and sends His angel Gabriel with a prophetic and frightening message.

Group Discussion:

Have you ever made a mistake that was so bad you were afraid to admit it? What happened when you owned up to your mistake? What did you learn?

Read Daniel 9:20-23 and answer the following questions:

1. When did Gabriel come to Daniel?

2. What did Gabriel come to give Daniel?

3. When was Gabriel given the order to appear before Daniel?

4. How did God view Daniel?

Gabriel comes to Daniel to give him a message from God and to give him an understanding of that message (Daniel 9:23). We have already discussed Daniel 9:24-27, but let's review it again by looking into the Word of God.

5. How many weeks were decreed for Daniel's people and Jerusalem?

6. What would these "weeks" accomplish?

"So you are to know and discern that from the issuing of a decree to restore and rebuild Jerusalem, until Messiah the Prince, there will be seven weeks and sixty-two weeks; it will be built again, with plaza and moat, even in times of distress." —Daniel 9:25 NASB

There is much debate about which king issued this decree: Cyrus, Darius or Artaxerxes. Even more confusing is which one was ruling at the time of the decree? The Bible says Darius the Mede took the throne from the Babylonians (Daniel 5:29-31). However, Daniel 6:28 implies that both Darius and Cyrus ruled at the same time. So which is it?

Cyrus' father was a Persian prince and his mother was the daughter of the king of Media. Around 550 B.C. Cyrus overthrew his grandfather, the king of Media, and became the king of both Media and Persia. When Babylon was invaded, Darius was placed in charge of Babylonia (or the Chaldeans) and became king there. Cyrus was king over all of Persia and Media, which today would have been parts of Turkey, Iran, and southern Iraq. The simplest way to interpret this is to think about our current form of government. In Canada, we have a prime minister and each province has a premier. In this scenario then, Cyrus would be the prime minister and Darius would be the premier. Now that you have a brief history and can see that both Cyrus and Darius reigned at the same time, we need to look at who issued the decree to restore and rebuild Jerusalem.

There are a few possibilities and I will present them all here. I am not a scholar, just a student of the Word like you. After much research, this is what I've found. First, I will present the order of the kings who reigned.

- Cyrus the Great reigned from 559 to 530 B.C.
- Cambyses reigned from 530 to 522 B.C.
- Darius the Great reigned from 522 to 486 B.C.
- Ahauserus (Xerxes I) reigned from 486 to 465 B.C.
- Artaxerxes I reigned from 465 to 424 B.C.
- Xerxes II reigned for 45 days in 424 B.C., before he was murdered by his brother Sogdianus.
- Sogdianus reigned from 424 to 423 B.C., and then he was assassinated by his brother Ochus (who took the name Darius II).

- Darius II reigned from 423 to 404 B.C.
- Artaxerxes II reigned from 404 to 358 B.C.

Of course, our concern is not who the kings were, but who issued the decree to restore and rebuild Jerusalem (Daniel 9:25). This list is to give you a better idea of the timeframe of when events happened in the Bible. I maintain that it was Cyrus the Great who issued the order to restore and rebuild Jerusalem. During my research, I found I wasn't alone in that belief. However, I believe those who disagree do so because they are hung up on one mistranslated word and date-setting.

They are relying on a Greek historian named Claudius Ptolemy. Ptolemy was an astronomer, mathematician, astrologer, and geographer who was born about 100 years after Christ. He wrote *The Canon of the Kings,* "which was a dated list of kings used by ancient astronomers as a convenient means to date astronomical phenomena, such as eclipses."[18] The canon originally came from Babylonian texts and it lists all Babylonian kings chronologically, starting from 747 B.C. It includes kings all the way to A.D. 160. It is this canon that today's archaeologists, astronomers, and Bible scholars rely on for dating. Which begs this question: why are biblical scholars not relying on the Scriptures but instead, trying to make a secular historian's dates fit into the prophetic timeline?

Yes, I understand the importance of the canon, but should it take precedence over scripture? Let's examine this date-setting in light of the Bible.

Why is King Cyrus, God's choice to rebuild the Temple and Jerusalem, rejected by scholars?

Most theologians reject King Cyrus because nothing in Daniel 9:25 mentions rebuilding the Temple. The verse, they insist, is about restoring and rebuilding Jerusalem *only.* They cite the following decree by Cyrus to prove their point:

*Thus says Cyrus king of Persia: "All the kingdoms of the earth the Lord God of heaven has given me. And **He has commanded me to build Him a house at Jerusalem** which is in Judah. Who is among you of all His people? May the Lord his God be with him, and let him go up!"* —2 Chronicles 36:23 NASB, emphasis mine

Because Cyrus mentions building a house (Temple) for the Lord and there is no mention of rebuilding Jerusalem, most theologians ignore the decree in Daniel 9:25. But I believe they have missed something important. They fail to take into account that Jerusalem is not Jerusalem without the Jewish Temple. In other words, to the Jews the Temple is Jerusalem. One cannot exist without the other.

They also ignore clear scriptural references that say Cyrus would rebuild the Temple and Jerusalem. In addition, according to Ptolemy's canon, if Cyrus issued the decree, it would not bring us to the time of Jesus. So Cyrus is written out of the equation.

Instead of Cyrus, most theologians believe it is Artaxerxes II who issued the command to restore and rebuild Jerusalem in 457 B.C. They believe it because the dates take us to the time of Jesus and because of Nehemiah. Nehemiah was the cupbearer to the king, and it was this king who gave him permission to rebuild the walls of Jerusalem (Nehemiah 1:1-4; 2:1-20). So who is right? Once again, we need to compare scripture with scripture, and we will start at the beginning of Daniel 9.

When Daniel discovers the seventy years of desolations predicted by the prophet Jeremiah were coming to an end (Daniel 9:1-19), he immediately begins to pray and confess the sins of his people to God and asks the Lord not to delay any longer in restoring the Jews to their city and Temple. While he is praying, the angel Gabriel is sent to him with an answer. Gabriel explains that a decree is going to be issued to restore and rebuild Jerusalem. This decree or proclamation would end the seventy years of that city's desolations. He also explains this same decree would begin a prophetic period of 490 years that God had determined would come upon the Jewish people and upon the city of Jerusalem. Who issued that decree? King Cyrus. His order officially ended the seventy years of desolation that had been predicted by Jeremiah.

Ezra 1:1-11 confirms that Cyrus was intent on building the house of the Lord. In addition, the Lord Himself confirmed that Cyrus would also rebuild Jerusalem:

"It is I who says of Cyrus, 'He is My shepherd! And he will perform all My desire.' **And he declares of Jerusalem, 'She will be built,' and of the Temple, 'Your foundation will be laid.'"** —Isaiah 44:28 NASB, emphasis mine

Clearly, the Lord declares Cyrus would rebuild both Jerusalem and the Temple. But theologians won't accept Cyrus because of the date he issued his decree, 538 B.C. This date is too early for the time of Jesus; so Cyrus is rejected. But are we to disregard Isaiah 44:28, which names Cyrus as the rebuilder of the Temple and Jerusalem? Even Isaiah 45:13 confirms God had chosen Cyrus (pre-ordained him) to rebuild the Temple as well as Jerusalem:

"I have aroused him in righteousness and I will make all his ways smooth. **He will build My city** *and will let My exiles go free, without any payment or reward," says the Lord of hosts.* —Isaiah 45:13 NASB, emphasis mine

The fact that Jerusalem and the Temple were not completed during Cyrus' reign further confirmed the belief in some that despite what the Bible said, King Cyrus did not fulfill Daniel 9:25.

However, Cyrus did issue the decree and many Jews set out to build their Temple. Unfortunately, they were met with opposition from those who had been living in the land during their seventy-year absence. In fact, they were met with resistance all the days of King Cyrus, right up until the reign of Darius the Great (Ezra 4:4-5). So it sounds like the Temple was not built in Cyrus' time and Jerusalem was not rebuilt either. However, I believe it would be more accurate to say the Temple and Jerusalem were not *finished* during Cyrus' time because of the opposition to the Jews rebuilding project.

The hostility to the Jews rebuilding their Temple was so great that the priests set up a temporary altar for burnt offerings but did not begin work on the Temple because they were terrified of the people in the area (Ezra 4:3). In fact, they constructed homes for themselves first before they even began work on the Temple. This went on for two years before God let them know, through the prophet Haggai, that He was not pleased.

[7]Thus says the Lord of hosts, "Consider your ways! [8]Go up to the mountains, bring wood and rebuild the Temple, that I may be pleased with it and be glorified," says the Lord. [9]"You look for much, but behold, it comes too little; when you bring it home, I blow it away. Why?" declares the Lord of hosts, "Because of My house which lies desolate, while each of you runs to his own house."—Haggai 1:7-9 NASB

The second king to issue a decree was King Darius the Great (Ezra 6:1-12). This was a confirmation of King Cyrus' decree for the people to get back to work on the Temple and for the other people there to stop oppressing the Jews so they could rebuild their Temple. It was on the twenty-fourth day of the sixth month in the second year of King Darius that work on the Temple began again in earnest (Haggai 1:15). The Temple was completed in the sixth year of the reign of King Darius the Great, around 515 B.C.

So the Temple is built, but Jerusalem is still in ruins. Therefore, King Darius' decree is ruled out by theologians. After King Darius died, those who opposed the Jews' rebuilding plans for Jerusalem rose up against them once again.

⁶Now in the reign of Ahasuerus, in the beginning of his reign, they wrote an accusation against the inhabitants of Judah and Jerusalem. ⁷And in the days of Artaxerxes, Bishlam, Mithredath, Tabeel and the rest of his colleagues wrote to Artaxerxes king of Persia; and the text of the letter was written in Aramaic and translated from Aramaic. —Ezra 4:6-7 NASB

We have two different kings mentioned in the above verse. This is not Ezra using two different names for one king. The first king, Ahasuerus (Xerxes I), was the same king mentioned in the book of Esther. The second king is Artaxerxes I whom, it would seem from Ezra 4:11-24, stopped the work in Jerusalem up until the reign of King Darius the Great. But how can that be since, according to the Scriptures, Darius I reigned *before* Artaxerxes I? The website "Apologetics Press" suggests the following:

One possible solution to this difficulty is that Ahasuerus and Artaxerxes of Ezra 4:6, 7-23 were respectively Cambyses (530-522) and Smerdis (522)— kings of Persia (listed above) who reigned before Darius I. Since Persian kings frequently had two or more names, it is not unfathomable to think that Cambyses and Smerdis also may have gone by the names Ahasuerus and Artaxerxes (see Wilson, 1996; see also Fausset, 1998).[19]

Another explanation to this perceived dilemma is that the information concerning the kings of Persia in Ezra 4 is grouped according to theme rather than by chronology. Instead of having a record where everything in chapter four is in sequential order, it is reasonable to conclude that verses 6-23 serve as a parenthetical comment and that Ahasuerus and Artaxerxes (4:6-7) are indeed Ahasuerus (486-465) and Artaxerxes I (465-424) of history (rather than the aforementioned Cambyses and Smerdis). (Eric Lyons)

The third king to issue a decree was Artaxerxes I. He made matters worse and commanded the Jews to stop rebuilding Jerusalem (Ezra 4:17-24) in response to a letter he received from those who opposed the rebuilding project:

"To King Artaxerxes: Your servants, the men in the region beyond the River, and now ¹²let it be known to the king that the Jews who came up from

you have come to us at Jerusalem; **they are rebuilding the rebellious and evil city and are finishing the walls and repairing the foundations.** *[13]Now let it be known to the king, that if that city is rebuilt and the walls are finished, they will not pay tribute, custom or toll, and it will damage the revenue of the kings. [14]Now because we are in the service of the palace, and it is not fitting for us to see the king's dishonor, therefore we have sent and informed the king, [15]so that a search may be made in the record books of your fathers. And you will discover in the record books and learn that that city is a rebellious city and damaging to kings and provinces, and that they have incited revolt within it in past days; therefore that city was laid waste. [16]We inform the king that if that city is rebuilt and the walls finished, as a result you will have no possession in the province beyond the River."—Ezra 4:11-16 NASB,* emphasis mine

Clearly, the Jews who had gone up to Jerusalem *originally,* during Cyrus' time, were still rebuilding the city (because the Temple was complete), just as King Cyrus had commanded back in his day. But after reading this letter, Artaxerxes stopped the building project. However, he did allow any Jews remaining in Babylon to travel to Jerusalem to worship at their Temple and he supplied them with everything they would need from the royal treasury (Ezra 7:11-26). This was not a command to restore or rebuild Jerusalem at all, but a decree to supply the house of God with what it needed from the royal treasury.

The fourth decree concerning Jerusalem was sent out by King Artaxerxes II. It is this king most historians believe fulfilled Daniel 9:25. For one reason, the date in which it was issued was 457 B.C. This date "worked" in regard to this line in Daniel 9:25, about "the Messiah":

*"So you are to know and discern that from the issuing of a decree to restore and rebuild Jerusalem **until Messiah the Prince** there will be seven weeks and sixty-two weeks; it will be built again, with plaza and moat, even in times of distress." (emphasis mine)*

You can see why scholars chose Artaxerxes II's decree. It "worked" because it brings us right up to Jesus' time.

So where does all that leave us? Do we ignore scripture that plainly says King Cyrus issued the decree to rebuild the Temple and Jerusalem or do we go with Artaxerxes II because his date is closer to the time of Jesus? Were the Temple and Jerusalem rebuilt during times of distress? Very much so. Even with each king's decree or permission given, opposition to the rebuilding of Jerusalem was extremely high. But which decree meets the Lord's timetable in regard to the coming of the Messiah? More importantly, does Daniel 9:25 even speak of the Messiah or is it someone else? We will talk about that in the next chapter.

LIFE APPLICATION: Sometimes it is difficult to discern the Scriptures when we have so many conflicting viewpoints. First Timothy 3:16-17 reminds us that all scripture is God-breathed. Yet, many Bible teachers want us to accept teachings that are not found in the Bible but based on man's opinions. How do you recognize the truth? Take some time today and ask God to show you His truths.

15. A JEWISH PERSPECTIVE

> *So you are to know and discern that from the issuing of a **decree** to restore and rebuild Jerusalem until **Messiah the Prince** there will be seven weeks and sixty-two weeks; it will be built again, with plaza and moat, even in times of distress.* —Daniel 9:25 NASB, emphasis mine
>
> *Know therefore and discern, that from the going forth of the **word** to restore and to build Jerusalem unto **one anointed, a prince**, shall be seven weeks; and for threescore and two weeks, it shall be built again, with broad place and moat, but in troublous times.* —Daniel 9:25 JPS, emphasis mine

In Daniel 9:25 the original Hebrew uses the word *dabar* for the word "decree," which is vastly different from a human decree. The word *dabar* refers to a "prophetic word." In the beginning of Daniel 9:2 for example, this word is used when Daniel says he wants to understand "the word (*dabar*) of the Lord to the Prophet Jeremiah." When King Cyrus issued his decree, the original Hebrew word used in Ezra 1:1 is *qōwl,* meaning "a proclamation or commandment." In fact, the word *dabar* (as it pertains to a prophetic word) is never used in any of the proclamations given by Cyrus, Darius or Artaxerxes.

Why is this important? It's important because the whole meaning of Daniel 9:25 changes and now reads:

*Know therefore and discern, that from the going forth of **the word** to restore and to build Jerusalem unto one anointed, a prince, shall be seven weeks.* —Daniel 9:25 JPS emphasis mine

In other words, from the time Jeremiah issued his prophetic word about the Jewish exile to Babylon lasting seventy years, until King Cyrus, there would be forty-nine years. When Jeremiah prophesied about the exile to Babylon, the year was

605 B.C. It was the first year of Nebuchadnezzar's reign (Jeremiah 25:1). The Jews had been in subjugation for approximately twenty-one years before Jeremiah issued his prophetic word (*dabar*) about how long they would be in Babylon. When King Cyrus issued his proclamation (*qōwl*), forty-nine years *after* Jeremiah's prophecy, the exile was complete, a total of seventy years. Now let's look at the rest of that verse from a Jewish perspective. Does any of it point to the Messiah as we've been taught?

Know therefore and discern, that from the going forth of the word to restore and to build Jerusalem unto **one anointed, a prince,** *shall be seven weeks.* — Daniel 9:25 JPS emphasis mine

Notice that the word Messiah is missing and replaced with "anointed" in the Jewish version of this verse. This is because the Jews never saw the word "Messiah" in their scriptures. They saw the word *mashiach*, which means "anointed." It comes from the root word *mashach*, which means to "smear, rub, spread a liquid, or anoint." It does not mean "Messiah" or "Saviour" as we Christians interpret it. It simply means "anointed," nothing more. In addition, you will notice that the JPS has the word "one" before the word "anointed," whereas, the NASB says "Messiah the Prince." The NIV translates this part as "the Anointed One" and places the word "one" after anointed. Why is this important?

The word *mashiach* is used throughout Jewish scriptures no less than 100 times and refers to individuals, places, and objects. For example, it refers to priests, kings, and prophets (Leviticus 4:3; 1 Kings 1:39; Isaiah 61:1). It also refers to anointed places like the Temple altar (Exodus 40:9-11) and anointed things like unleavened bread (Numbers 6:15). And finally, it refers to King Cyrus, a non-Jewish King (Isaiah 45:1).

In Christian Bibles, 99 percent of the time, *mashiach* is translated as "anointed," with two exceptions: Daniel 9:25 and

26. So the question one has to ask is this: why? Especially since in Daniel 9:24, *mashiach* was correctly translated as "anointed." This does not make sense. It is inconsistent. You cannot translate *mashiach* to mean "anointed" *in the entire Bible* and then translate it to mean "Messiah" in two verses. I cannot explain why this was done. It's as if those who originally translated this part of Daniel imposed their own Christian beliefs about what the verse actually means. I am not a linguist, but even I can see that something is odd here. How does one word translate to mean "anointed" everywhere else in the Christian Bible, but in Daniel 9:25-26 it translates as "the Messiah"? When you read the Torah (the Jewish Bible), it is immediately clear it has not been changed in this way.

I believe this is why the Jewish people get so upset with our interpretation of their scriptures. Imagine the audacity it takes to say to a Jewish person who speaks and reads Hebrew that they aren't reading or interpreting their own scriptures correctly. That's like trying to tell a Christian that Jesus didn't die for their sins and He never existed. They would be adamant they are right, just as the Jews are adamant about their scriptures and the interpretation of them. We need to respect that and stop seeing things that aren't there.

Daniel 9:25 should read as "until an anointed prince" and not as "until Messiah the prince." And Daniel 9:26 should read, "An anointed one will be cut off" and not, "The Messiah will be cut off."

Now, let's look at this entire section one more time to be clear on what it says and means. My comments are in brackets:

24 Seventy weeks (490 years) *are decreed upon thy people and upon thy holy city, to finish the transgression* (rebellion against God) *and to make an end of sin* (sin offering), *and to forgive iniquity, and to bring in everlasting righteousness* (worship at the Temple), *and to seal vision and prophet* (Daniel), *and to anoint the most holy place* (Holy of Holies).

> [25]*Know therefore and discern, that from the going forth of the word* (Jeremiah's prophetic word) *to restore and to build Jerusalem unto one anointed, a prince,* (King Cyrus) *shall be seven weeks* (forty-nine years); *and for threescore and two weeks* (434 years), *it shall be built again, with broad place and moat, but in troublous times.*
>
> [26] *And after the threescore and two weeks* (sixty-two weeks, 434 years) *shall an anointed one be cut off, and be no more* (the Jews believe this is in reference to Onias III, a high priest who was assassinated for opposing the Hellenization of the Temple); *and the people of a prince that shall come* (Antiochus Epiphanes IV) *shall destroy the city and the sanctuary; but his end shall be with a flood; and unto the end of the war desolations are determined.*
>
> [27] *And he* (Antiochus) *shall make a firm covenant with many for one week* (seven years); *and for half of the week* (three and half years) *he shall cause the sacrifice and the offering to cease; and upon the wing of detestable things shall be that which causeth appalment* (idol in the Temple); *and that until the extermination wholly determined be poured out upon that which causeth appalment.* —Daniel 9:24-27 JPS

Seven weeks is forty-nine years. Sixty-two weeks is 434 years. That gives us 483 years. According to secular documents, Cyrus issued his decree in 538 B.C., which brings us to 55 B.C., about eighty years too early for Jesus' appearance. This is why Artaxerxes II is the king who most scholars believe gave the commandment to rebuild Jerusalem. Artaxerxes gave the order sometime around 457 B.C. And if we start at 457 B.C. for the "going forth of the commandment to restore and to build Jerusalem," the 483 years brings us to about A.D.26, which is very near the time when Jesus began his public ministry. Unfortunately, because Bible translators changed *mashiach* from "anointed" to "Messiah" they have placed more meaning on this verse than is there. In short, I believe Daniel 9:24-25 has nothing to do with Jesus at all.

In the last chapter we discovered that some theologians disregard King Cyrus for issuing the commandment to restore and rebuild the Temple and Jerusalem because he doesn't fit into the timeline for Jesus' appearance. We also discovered that scripture confirmed Cyrus was the one whom God chose to issue the decree to rebuild the Temple and Jerusalem. Yet, these vital verses are ignored by many.

In today's chapter we learned that the word for "anointed" is *mashiach*. We also learned that throughout the entire Christian Bible this word is translated as "anointed," but in two verses (Daniel 9:25-26) it is changed to mean something else. For me that is a red flag that needs to be addressed. Is it possible that early Christian translators were imposing their own beliefs into what this passage actually means? We will discover that as we move on with this study.

One thing we need to remember is that Cyrus did issue a decree, the anointed one did come and was cut off, and Jerusalem fell. We will talk about whom that anointed one was in our next lesson.

LIFE APPLICATION: Finding deeper truths in the Bible is what this study is all about. You have just read (maybe for the first time) that what is generally accepted as fact in Daniel 9:24-27 may not be the case. I'll admit when the Lord first led me to this discovery, it took some time for me to accept it. So today, if you have the time, do a little research of your own. Discuss this chapter with your friends, family, and maybe even your pastor. Read some commentaries and ask the Lord to reveal His truth to you. Don't take my word for it. Search the Scriptures for yourself.

16. IS IT PAST OR IS IT FUTURE?

[15]Therefore when you see the ABOMINATION OF DESOLATION which was spoken of through Daniel the prophet, standing in the holy place (let the reader understand), [16] then those who are in Judea must flee to the mountains.
—Matthew 24:15-16 NASB

When Jesus warned His disciples about the abomination of desolation, was His warning for the people of His day alone or was He warning us as well? As previously discussed, Antiochus Epiphanes IV had already conquered Jerusalem and desecrated the Temple *before* Jesus came on the scene. But Jesus knew the Temple would be destroyed in A.D. 70, almost forty years after His death and resurrection. So were His warnings for the people of His day alone or have Christians been reading something into Daniel and the seventy weeks that isn't there? Is it possible that the dates and timing we discussed—in regard to when Cyrus issued the decree—do not have anything to do with the Messiah at all? Were Christians so desperate to make Daniel 9 about Jesus that they had to keep moving the dates when the decree was issued to restore and rebuild Jerusalem to Artaxerxes II to make it work? I'm asking these questions because they need to be addressed.

Was there anyone, besides Antiochus, who entered the Temple and desecrated it like he did? Caligula ordered that a statue of himself be erected for worship in the Temple in A.D. 40, but his subsequent assassination prevented that from happening. In A.D. 63, General Pompey did enter the Holy of Holies but was so awestruck by it that he quickly left, ordered it cleansed, and reinstated Temple sacrifices. In A.D. 70, when the Temple was destroyed, no one entered it. Instead, it was burned to the ground. However, Roman soldiers were all over the Temple Mount area. So would that alone have been considered an "abomination of desolation?" How did the Jews of Jesus' day view the Roman invasion onto their Temple Mount? How do they view it today with the Muslims there? It is very important that we find the answer to this because it plays a huge part on whether or not Daniel 9:26-27 is in our past or our future. Have Christians been misinterpreting Daniel 9:26-27? Let's find out by looking at it from a Jewish perspective. First, let's compare the Jewish Publication Society's 1917 edition of the Torah with the NASB (New American Standard Bible).

[26] *"And after the threescore and two weeks shall **an anointed one** be cut off, **and be no more;** and the people of **a prince** that shall come shall destroy the city and the sanctuary; but **his end** shall be with a flood; and unto **the end of the war** desolations are determined.* [27] *And he shall make a firm covenant with many for one week; and for half of the week he shall cause the sacrifice and the offering to cease; **and upon the wing of detestable things shall be that which causeth appalment;** and that until the extermination wholly determined **be poured out upon that which causeth appalment."** —Daniel 9:26-27 JPS emphasis mine*

[26] *"Then after the sixty-two weeks **the Messiah** will be cut off **and have nothing** and the people of **the prince** who is to come will destroy the city and the sanctuary. **And its end** will come with a flood; **even to the end there will be war;** desolations are determined.* [27] *And he will make a firm covenant with the many for one week, but in the middle of the week he will put a stop to sacrifice and grain offering; and on **the wing of abominations will come one who makes desolate,** even until a complete destruction, one that is decreed, is **poured out on the one who makes desolate."** —Daniel 9:26-27 NASB emphasis mine*

As you can see, the differences between the two versions are astounding and each has a different meaning altogether. One is a prophetic prediction of Antiochus Epiphanes IV. The other predicts the Messiah's coming and the Antichrist in our future. So which one is right?

Group Discussion:

Is Daniel 9:26-27 in our future, past or both?

Using the verses above, answer the following questions:

1. In the NASB translation, "the anointed one" is named as the Messiah. What happens to him?

2. What happens to "the anointed one" in the JPS version?

3. What do the people of "the prince who is to come" do? What is destroyed?

4. Once again comparing the JPS to the NASB, whose (or what) end will "come with a flood"? Do you see a difference?

5. What does the prince agree to do for the many and for how long?

6. Keeping in mind that "one week" is seven years, what happens midway through the covenant? What does the prince do?

The NASB says, "On the wing of abominations *will come* one who makes desolate" (emphasis mine). The JPS says, "Upon the wing of detestable things *shall be that* which causeth appalment" (emphasis mine). Now I'm going to throw one more translation into the mix. The KJV reads, "For the overspreading of abominations *he shall make it* desolate" (emphasis mine).

Clearly, something that is detestable to the Jews would cause them utter and complete horror. The KJV uses the literal term "overspreading of abominations," letting the reader know and understand that in addition to this "prince" stopping the sacrifices and offerings, "on the wing of that" —or in addition to that—he sets up something (probably an idol) in the Temple, making it desolate, or as the JPS says, causing appalment to the Jews. We know this very thing happened with Antiochus Epiphanes IV when he set up an idol of Zeus (made to look like him) and slew a pig on the altar in the Temple. Josephus Flavius says the following of Antiochus:

He also spoiled the Temple, and put a stop to the constant practice of offering a daily sacrifice of expiation for three years and six months.[20]

It is important to note that this three-and-a-half-year period did happen with Antiochus during his seven-year reign of terror over Jerusalem.

Two books that should be viewed as historical (not divinely inspired by God) are the first and second books of the Maccabees. These historical books back up what Josephus wrote but also affirm the war the Jews had with Antiochus Epiphanes IV. They also give us the dates when certain things happened in history.

Before I continue I want to be clear that even if Antiochus fulfills the prophecy of Daniel 9:26-27, that does not mean it didn't or won't happen again. In Matthew 24:15 Jesus said it would happen again, and His prediction came true in A.D. 70 when the most abominable thing happened: the destruction of the Temple. However, even its destruction did not stop others from desecrating the area where it once stood.

In A.D. 137, Roman Emperor Hadrian erected a Temple of Jupiter on the Temple Mount, as well as a statue of himself, in response to the Jewish attempt to rebuild a third Temple. Clearly, when Jesus warned about the abomination that causes desolation, He wasn't referring to a one-time incident. Anything erected on the Temple Mount that is not honouring to God is an abomination of desolation. Therefore, we can rightly assume that the current Al Aqsa Mosque and the Dome of the Rock are an abomination of desolation to the Jews. The only reason that mosque is there is to prevent the Jews from rebuilding their Temple. While Muslims say the area is sacred to them, it really is not. There are many examples of how they really feel about the area. While Jews pray facing Jerusalem and their sacred Temple Mount, Muslims pray toward the city of Mecca in Saudi Arabia, with their behinds pointed at their "sacred mosque."

They also use the Temple Mount area as a playground where they have picnics and play soccer. They do not treat it as a sacred place.

In 2009 Sari Nusseibeh, a Palestinian professor and president of Al Quds University, admitted in the book *Where Heaven and Earth Meet: Jerusalem's Sacred Esplanade* that the Temple Mount was a Jewish holy site before Muslims stepped foot there. As a result of this admission, he was (according to the Israeli Daily Ma'ariv) threatened by Palestinians.[21]

Ibn Taymiyyah (1263-1328) was an important Islamic scholar who wrote that "Sacred Islamic sites are to be found only in the Arabian Peninsula" and "In Jerusalem there is not a place one calls sacred and the same holds true for the tombs of Hebron."[22] Deep down, Muslims know they are occupying a Jewish holy site. They are so disrespectful of their supposedly sacred Dome of the Rock that from time to time, they start riots on the Temple Mount and actually vandalize their own mosque. You can see footage of this vandalism on YouTube.[23]

The Dome of the Rock is not sacred to Muslims at all. It is merely a deterrent to the Jews to rebuilding their Temple. In addition to all that, Jerusalem is not even sacred to Muslims. It is mentioned in the Quran zero times, but in the Bible, it is mentioned 667 times. If Jerusalem were important to Muslims, it should be mentioned in the Quran at least once. However, the Holy Land (Israel) is written about in the Quran as the land that was given by Allah to the Jews and even tells that the Jews will return to their land (Sura 5:20-21; Sura 7:137; Sura 7:144). Clearly, Muslims have no claim to Jerusalem, the Temple Mount or Israel. So is there an abomination of desolation on the Temple Mount today? I'll leave that up to you.

Is Daniel 9:26-27 a prophecy concerning Antiochus or is it a future Antichrist with a seven-year peace treaty still to come as we've been taught? Jesus did not say anything about a future Antichrist. He warned that there would be false prophets who would arise and who would deceive many (Matthew 24:11). But He never said a future man known as the Antichrist would appear. He only warned about an abomination of desolation and future tribulation. In order to look at the Scriptures historically and accurately, we must not be biased based on what we've been taught for years. So let's take a closer look, using the dates set forth in the books of the Maccabees, to see if Antiochus Epiphanes IV fulfills the prophecy of Daniel 9:26-27. Is there a future seven-year period when an Antichrist will make a peace treaty with the Jews and then, halfway through, break it? Or has it already been fulfilled? The following table gives us a clear image of these events in history.

Timeline of Antiochus Epiphanes IV

Dates	Verse	Event
175 B.C.	1 Maccabees 1:10	Antiochus begins his reign.
171 B.C.	1 Maccabees 1:10-15	In order to placate Antiochus, Hellenized Jews agree to a peace covenant with Antiochus to worship Greek gods.
171-170 B.C.	2 Maccabees 4:7-18 1 Maccabees 1:16-19	Sacrifices are neglected. Priests abandon worship of God in favour of idols. Antiochus plunders Egypt.
169 B.C.	1 Maccabees 1:20-28	Antiochus plunders the Temple.
167 B.C.	1 Maccabees 1:29-64 2 Maccabees 6:1-2	Sacrifices stopped, Jerusalem plundered, all Jewish practices stopped, desolating image set up in Temple, pig sacrificed on altar in Temple, Jews forced to partake in horrible acts or die.
166 B.C.	1 Maccabees 3-4	Maccabean revolt.
164 B.C	1 Maccabees 4:42-58 2 Maccabees 10:1-8	Temple cleansed, Antiochus dies.

As you can see, starting from the time the peace treaty was made between the Hellenized Jews in 171 B.C. and Antiochus' death, there were seven years. Midway through the treaty all sacrifices stopped, Jerusalem was plundered, and Antiochus ordered a pig be sacrificed on the altar and a statue of himself (as Zeus) be erected for worship. The entire defilement lasted 1,150 (2,300 evenings and mornings) days, or three and a half years, as written in Daniel 8:14.

> [13] *Then I heard a holy one speaking, and another holy one said to that particular one who was speaking, "How long will the vision about the regular sacrifice apply, while the transgression causes horror, so as to allow both the holy place and the host to be trampled?"* [14] *He said to me, "For 2,300 evenings and mornings; then the holy place will be properly restored."* —Daniel 8:13-14 NASB

It seems apparent from history that the prophecies regarding a future Antichrist were fulfilled in Antiochus.

But what about Jesus' warning that this would happen again?

> [15] *Therefore when you see the ABMONIATION OF DESOLATION which was spoken of through Daniel the prophet, standing in the holy place (let the reader understand),* [16] *then those who are in Judea must flee to the mountains.* —Matthew 24:15-16 NASB

Was the abomination of desolation the total destruction of the Temple in A.D. 70? We know from the eye witness account of Jewish historian Josephus Flavius that when the Jews saw the Temple go up in flames, they were horrified. So much so that even though it meant certain death, they rushed toward the Temple in an attempt to save it. And Jesus had even warned them not to do that in Matthew 24:15-20.

Was the abomination that causes desolation the end of the Temple as the Jewish people knew it? Or was it the Roman soldiers who trespassed in the Temple area, who were so close to the Holy of Holies that they were able to start a fire in it? Or was it a combination of both? Or is it still in our future?

So far, history seems to indicate that Antiochus was the fulfillment of these verses. However, we are not finished studying Daniel yet. We have so much more to discover, and I know, with God's help, we will be shown the truth.

LIFE APPLICATION: Uncovering truths in the Scriptures is like working on a jigsaw puzzle. Once you have all the right pieces together, everything suddenly fits. Prophecy must always be studied contextually and historically to be able to uncover its meaning. Today, pray about what you've learned and then ask the Lord to keep you grounded in His truths, not mine.

17. UNSEEN FORCES

After Daniel's vision in chapter nine, he jumps back in time (Daniel 10:1) to talk about a vision he had during the third year of Cyrus King of Persia. He explains how it left him: *"In those days, I, Daniel, had been mourning for three entire weeks. I did not eat any tasty food, nor did meat or wine enter my mouth, nor did I use any ointment at all until the entire three weeks were completed"* (Daniel 10:2-3 NASB). Daniel has been left reeling over what he saw. But we are not told about the vision or what he saw until chapter eleven, and it is related by an angel who Daniel does not name.

Group Discussion:

If you could time travel, would you visit your past or your future? Why?

Read Daniel 10:1-21 and answer the following questions:

1. In chapter ten we get more information about when Daniel had his vision. Who does Daniel say was reigning?

2. How long did Daniel mourn after the vision?

3. On the twenty-fourth day of the first month (Nissan), Daniel had a vision. Describe what he saw.

4. Read Daniel 8:15-16 and Daniel 9:20-21. Compare Daniel's descriptions and reactions to Gabriel with the vision he sees in Daniel 10:4-6. Was this being Gabriel?

The reaction Daniel had to this being is very different isn't it? The *NIV Quest Study Bible* has the following suggestion on who it could be:

Who was this man? Probably an angel—perhaps Gabriel, who had visited Daniel before (8:16). Some suggest the man was Christ, given the similar description in Revelation 1:12–16. But it seems unlikely that Christ would need help from the angel Michael (10:13) in a spiritual battle.

5. Daniel said he alone saw the vision. The men who were with him did not see it. What did they do? How did they react?

6. How did the angel refer to Daniel? What did he call him?

7. One touch by the angel seems to strengthen Daniel enough to stand (Daniel 10:12). Why did the angel come to him?

> [13] *But the prince of the kingdom of Persia was withstanding me for twenty-one days; then behold, Michael, one of the chief princes, came to help me, for I had been left there with the kings of Persia. —Daniel 10:13 NASB*

Who is this "prince of the kingdom of Persia"? Strong's H8269 translates the word "prince" into the Hebrew word *sar*, which has many meanings: "prince, ruler, chief, captain, leader," and quite a few other forms of leadership. It can be in reference to an earthly leader or an unearthly one, as we see in the second half of the verse above, where the archangel Michael is referred to as the "chief of princes." Hebrew words have many meanings. When I looked up the Hebrew definition of the word "prince," I also discovered the word *sar* was used in reference to the prince of darkness or Satan. This gives us a better understanding of the prince of the kingdom of Persia. The angel Daniel was talking to had been fighting, or withstanding the prince of the kingdom of Persia (Satan), for twenty-one days. However, it is clear that this unnamed angel could not defeat this "prince" until the archangel Michael intervened. It would seem that even the prince of darkness must obey the "chief of princes," the archangel Michael.

After the angel touches Daniel's lips, he is able to talk. And Daniel tells him it is the vision that has left him in anguish without any strength. He is shaken so badly by the vision (and no doubt the angel's appearance) he literally has the breath knocked out of him (vv. 16-17). But the angel sees how badly shaken Daniel is and touches him again and once more strengthens him.

8. The angel said he came to give Daniel understanding as to what would happen to his people in the future. What was Daniel's reaction to that?

Daniel was incredibly upset by the vision he'd had and so distraught by what he knew was coming that he was in mourning for three weeks. What I like about this chapter is the love and care God shows for Daniel by sending one of His angels to strengthen him during this time. This was one of the reasons the angel visited him, to give him courage and to strengthen him for what was to come.

The angel leaves Daniel and tells him he is going to fight against the prince of Persia. If you ever wondered about events unfolding in the spiritual realm where we can't see, this is a great example of such an event. These "princes" the angelic being talks about in regard to Persia and Greece are satanic beings. We know this because Michael, who is the chief prince or archangel of God, was fighting against them with this unnamed angel (whom some believe to be Gabriel) who came to strengthen Daniel.

For our struggle is not against flesh and blood, but against the rulers, against the authorities, against the powers of this dark world and against the spiritual forces of evil in the heavenly realms. —Ephesians 6:12 NIV

The veil has been pulled back for Daniel and for us so that we might be able to see what is going on behind the scenes. The Persian rule is about to end and the Greek Empire is about to rise and will play a huge part in fulfilling prophecy. The next two chapters reveal what is to come.

LIFE APPLICATION: We have no idea what is going on in the spiritual realm on our behalf. Think about the people you meet during your day. Why have they been placed in your path? There are no coincidences in a Christian's life. Everything has a purpose and a reason—even the bad stuff. Think about your current situation. In my own life, I have many health problems that have left me disabled. But I personally believe God has ordained me to have these problems for a reason: to be an encouragement to those who are suffering. What about you? How has God been moving in your life? Take some time today and ask Him to show you where you can best serve Him.

18. KINGS OF THE NORTH AND SOUTH (PART 1)

Daniel has been strengthened by a heavenly being sent from God and now this angelic being reveals even more to Daniel about what will happen to his people. You will see as we discuss the next chapters that most of it is in our past. Today we will look closely at the Scriptures along with history to see where things are in Daniel's timeline and ours.

Group Discussion:

Do you believe history repeats itself?

Read Daniel 11:1-35 and answer the following questions. Keep in mind that this is the angel from the previous chapter speaking. He is revealing to Daniel what is to take place in the future.

1. This angel is revealing more than just the future. In the first verse, what does he reveal about his presence? Who did he come to encourage and protect?

2. How many more kings were going to arise in Persia?

3. What is special about the fourth king?

4. After he becomes strong, what does he do?

5. After the fourth king of Persia, another mighty king will arise. What happens to his kingdom?

History and the Bible reveal that three more kings did arise in Persia. Their names were Ahasuerus (also known as Xerxes and Cambysses, Ezra 4:6); Artaxerxes 1 (Ezra 4:7) and Darius the Great (not to be confused with Darius the Mede, Ezra 4:24). Then a fourth king would arise and gain far more riches than all the kings of Persia before him. He was known as Xerxes the Great. He invaded Greece from 483 to 480 B.C.

6. A mighty king arises (Daniel 11:3). What will his rule be like?

7. What happens to his kingdom?

8. Did his kingdom go to his own descendants?

In Daniel 11:3-4 we learn of a mighty king who will arise, whose kingdom will be divided up to the "four-points of the compass, though not to his own descendants." History proves this was Alexander the Great. After his death, his kingdom was split four ways, not to his own descendants but to his generals, as I previously discussed.

But now we run into some confusing scripture because from here it is all somewhat cryptic. For example, the king of the south and the king of the north are not named. So once again we have to look to the Scriptures and history to find out who they were. This is where many Bible teachers believe that the kings of the south and north are future "end-times" kings. However, we can verify through history and God's Word that these kings are in our past.

Then the King of the South will grow strong, along with one of his princes who will gain ascendancy over him and obtain dominion; his domain will be a great dominion indeed. —Daniel 11:5 NASB

One of the first things to remember when thinking about north and south in the Bible is that Jerusalem is the centre of the compass. Therefore, the Seleucid dynasty, whose capital was in Syria, was the king of the north, because Syria is north of

Jerusalem. The Ptolemaic dynasty represented the king of the south, because his capital was in Egypt, south of Jerusalem.

9. The king of the south tries to form an alliance with the king of the north. What does he do (Daniel 11:5-6)?

10. Does the peace between the two nations last?

After many battles between all four kingdoms (Ptolemaic, Antogonid, Seleucid, and Attalid) for supremacy, two empires remained: the Seleucid king in the north and the Ptolemaic king in the south. Philetaerus, who established the Attalid Empire, which was really just the fortified city of Pergamum, quickly pledged allegiance to Seleucus and was absorbed into the Seleucid Empire when Seleucus I killed Lysimachus (Antigonus' successor of the Antogonid Empire) in battle in 281B.C.[24] Now two dynasties remained in Alexander's old empire.

After some years they will form an alliance, and the daughter of the King of the South will come to the King of the North to carry out a peaceful arrangement. But she will not retain her position of power, nor will he remain with his power, but she will be given up, along with those who brought her in and the one who sired her as well as he who supported her in those times. —Daniel 11:6 NASB

Around 249 B.C. the King of the South, Ptolemy II Philadelphus, offered his daughter Berenice in marriage to

Antiochus II Theos.[25] His goal was to stop the second Syrian war and unite the two kingdoms through marriage. However, there was one slight problem: Antiochus II Theos was already married. Of course that proved no problem for the king, who promptly exiled his wife, Laodice, to Ephesus and married Berenice. He also received an enormous dowry that I'm sure was another reason he agreed to the arrangement. Berenice, for her part in the plan, then convinced Antiochus II to reject Laodice's children and set up her own to succeed him on the throne.[26]

But just like the Scriptures predicted, she did not retain her position of power. Antiochus II eventually rejected her too in order to go back to his wife Laodice.[27] Sounds like a soap opera, doesn't it? Wait! It gets worse.

After Ptolemy II died in 246 B.C., Antiochus II left Berenice and their infant son in Antioch to live again with Laodice in Asia Minor. Laodice then took the occasion to poison her cheating husband, declare her son (Seleucus II Callinicus) king as soon as Antiochus II died, and then had Berenice and her infant son murdered. So, just as the prophecy said would happen, Ptolemy II Philadelphus, king of the south, along with his daughter Berenice, and Antiochus II Theos, king of the north, all lost in their struggle for power.

So far history and the Bible are right on track. So what happened next?

> [7]But one of the descendants of her line will arise in his place, and he will come against their army and enter the fortress of the King of the North, and he will deal with them and display great strength. [8]Also their gods with their metal images and their precious vessels of silver and gold he will take into captivity to Egypt, and he on his part will refrain from attacking the King of the North for some years. —Daniel 11:7-8 NASB

Who was this descendant? Ptolemy III Euergetes,[28] the eldest son of Ptolemy II and the brother of Berenice. So if your sister was murdered by your rival, what would you do? Invade their kingdom of course! That is exactly what Ptolemy III Euergetes did. His armies defeated the forces of the new king of the north (Seleucus II Callinicus), who was the son of Antiochus II and Laodice. Ptolemy III was successful in his campaign and captured and put to death Laodice. He showed his strength and fulfilled Daniel 11:7.

But did he take all the gods of the king of the north to Egypt and did he refrain from attacking them further? Let's find out.

During the third Syrian war, Ptolemy III (king of the south) recovered many of the sacred statues that the Persian forces of Cambyses (Ahasuerus from Ezra 4-6) had taken during their conquest of Egypt 300 years earlier. He acquired so much gold and silver during his campaign that he received 1,500 talents of silver annually as tribute from Seleucia (about 10 percent of his annual income). This annual tribute from the king of the north to the king of the south kept Ptolemy III from attacking Seleucus II for many years. [29]

Then the latter will enter the realm of the King of the South, but will return to his own land. —Daniel 11:9 NASB

Humiliated by his defeat at the hands of Ptolemy III, Seleucus II tried to invade Egypt but failed because his fleet was lost in a storm. Ptolemy III outlived Seleucus II by four or five years. He died after a fall from his horse. But Seleucus II had sons and the Scriptures and history once again verify that they wanted to avenge their father's humiliation.

His sons will mobilize and assemble a multitude of great forces; and one of them will keep on coming and overflow and pass through, that he may again wage war up to his very fortress. —Daniel 11:10 NASB

The sons of Seleucus were Seleucus III and Antiochus III the Great. Seleucus III was the eldest and became king immediately upon his father's death. He, together with his brother Antiochus

III, began a war against the king of the south once again. But he was assassinated by members of his own army in 223 B.C. As a result, Antiochus III the Great ascended the throne at the ripe old age of 18. Around 219-218 B.C., Antiochus III marched his troops through Judea, coming very close to the borders of Egypt. And this made the king of the south, Ptolemy IV, furious and resulted in one of the largest battles ever fought in the ancient world. It was called the Battle of Raphia.[30]

The King of the South will be enraged and go forth and fight with the King of the North. Then the latter will raise a great multitude, but that multitude will be given into the hand of the former. —Daniel 11:11 NASB

According to Polybius, an ancient Greek historian, Ptolemy had 70,000 infantry, 5,000 cavalry, and 73 war elephants. Antiochus had 62,000 infantry, 6,000 cavalry, and 102 elephants.[31] But just like the angel predicted in Daniel 11:11, the king of the south, Ptolemy IV, defeated the king of the north, Antiochus III, in battle.

But things didn't end there. However, our lesson for today will. This is getting far too long and confusing. I'm sorry to bombard you with this history lesson. But it is vital because so far history and the Scriptures have proven that the kings of the north and south are in our past, not our future. Will they rise again? We'll find out in future lessons.

LIFE APPLICATION: It is clear the Lord had a plan that He laid out in perfect detail to Daniel. So far, everything the angel said would happen has been fulfilled. Jeremiah 29:10-14 says God had a plan for Israel. The reason behind it was simple: so the Jewish people would turn back to Him. Many people use Jeremiah 29:11 as a memory verse. It is my favourite because it helps me remember it isn't just the Jewish people God had a plan for. He had a plan for the whole human race. That plan was fulfilled in Jesus. Today, reflect on these verses and ask God if you are following His plans for you. So many times we think we are on the right path, but sometimes because of our own ambitions and dreams, we wander off the path God has set before us. Take some time now to make sure you are following God's plans and not your own.

19. KINGS OF THE NORTH AND SOUTH (PART 2)

How do we know God is omnipotent? Daniel 11 is so precise about events that would happen in the future that only the King of the universe would know what was going to happen. Of course there are those in the secular realm who believe Daniel was so precise in its predictions because they must have been written *after* the events. Modern scholars don't believe the book of Daniel was written by Daniel at all. They believe the stories of the first half were legendary in origin and the visions of the second half, the product of anonymous authors in the Maccabean period. They refuse to believe prophecy could be so accurate.

In fact, if you read a Catholic Bible, you will find chapters added to Daniel that you will not find in a Protestant Bible or even in the Torah. These additions are called the Apocrypha and were never acknowledged as inspired scripture by the Jews or by Jesus and the apostles. Jesus argued with the spiritual leaders of His day many times, but He never once quoted from the Apocrypha. He always quoted from the Torah, which is what Protestant Bibles base their canon of Scripture on. In addition, "the Dead Sea scrolls provide no commentary on the Apocrypha but do provide commentary on some of the Jewish Old Testament books. This probably indicates that the Jewish Essene community did not regard the Apocrypha as authoritative either."[32] Even Josephus did not quote from the Apocrypha. Clearly, Daniel's precise predictions are a stumbling block to those who refuse to believe in God or prophecy.

Fortunately, we do not have that stumbling block because we believe the Bible is the inspired Word of God. Today, we will continue to look at the angel's revelations to Daniel about what was going to happen in the future.

Group Discussion:

When we forget to include God in our plans, sometimes the results can be disastrous. Pride and ambition can so easily distract a Christian in this world of opportunities. What happens when we don't consult God about our plans, goals, dreams or even ideas?

Read Daniel 11:11-19 and answer the following questions. We will look at history and the Scriptures once again to see how these verses played out.

1. The king of the south went out to fight the king of the north. Describe what happened.

2. When the king of the south realizes his victory, he becomes proud and causes thousands to die, but he doesn't prevail. Why?

The largest battle in ancient history (the Battle of Raphia) occurred when the king of the south (Ptolemy IV Philopater) became enraged at the king of the north (Antiochus III). Scripture says:

[11]The King of the South will be enraged and go forth and fight with the King of the north. Then the latter will raise a great multitude, but that multitude will be given into the hand of the former. [12]When the multitude is carried away, his heart will be lifted up, and he will cause tens of thousands to fall; yet he will not prevail. [13]For the King of the north will again raise a greater multitude than the former, and after an interval of some years he will press on with a great army and much equipment. —Daniel 11:11-13 NASB

Antiochus III did raise a great multitude. As I stated in our last lesson, Ptolemy had 70,000 infantry, 5,000 cavalry, and 73 war elephants, and Antiochus had 62,000 infantry, 6,000 cavalry, and 102 elephants. But even though Antiochus' army was greater, he was defeated by Ptolemy IV. Ptolemy IV did cause tens of thousands to fall, but he was so proud of what had happened during the battle of Raphia that all he wanted to do was get back home to Alexandria, Egypt, and celebrate. However, in his haste to return home, he made two mistakes: he left the port of Seleucia-in-Pieria (which his father had captured) in the hands of Antiochus III. He also had trained his Egyptian troops how to fight. So when he returned home, those same troops began a successful guerilla campaign against his rule in Egypt. By the end of his reign, they had achieved total independence, leading to the secession of Upper Egypt that lasted nearly twenty years.[33]

3. Daniel 11:14 says many will rise against the king of the south. This includes Daniel's people (the Jews). What happens to them during this rebellion?

> *"Now in those times many will rise up against the King of the South; the violent ones among your people will also lift themselves up in order to fulfill the vision, but they will fall down.* [15] *Then the King of the North will come, cast up a siege ramp and capture a well-fortified city; and the forces of the South will not stand their ground, not even their choicest troops, for there will be no strength to make a stand.* [16]*But he who comes against him will do as he pleases, and no one will be able to withstand him; he will also stay for a time in the Beautiful Land, with destruction in his hand."* —Daniel 11:14-16 NASB

Eventually, Ptolemy IV died and his son Ptolemy V took the throne at the tender age of five. Due to his age, a bloody conflict ensued as to who would serve as regent until the king came of age. His mother was murdered and the regency was passed from one advisor to another until the kingdom was in a state of near anarchy. This is when the king of the north (Antiochus III) took advantage of the turmoil and "delivered a crushing blow to the Ptolemys at the Battle of Panium (Fifth Syrian War, 202-195 B.C.) which earned him the important port of Sidon."[34] The Battle of Panium marked the end of Ptolemaic rule in Judea.[35] Antiochus III retook the territory he had occupied some eighteen years previous. However, when he withdrew for the winter, the Egyptian commander Scopas reconquered the southern portions of the lost territory, including Judea and Jerusalem.

According to Jewish historian Josephus Flavius, the Jews went to Antiochus III of their own accord, received him into Jerusalem, provided his army with provisions, and assisted him when he besieged the garrison that was in Jerusalem.[36] Antiochus III, unlike his successor, Antiochus Epiphanes IV, rewarded the Jews and treated them kindly throughout his reign.

Following his defeat at the Battle of Panium, the Egyptian Commander Scopas fled to the fortified port city of Sidon. As the Bible indicates, Antiochus III (king of the north) besieged it, and in 199 B.C., in exchange for safe passage out of the city back to Egypt, Scopas surrendered.[37]

With the king of the south's total surrender, Antiochus III took the Holy Land away from the Egyptians. Judea and Jerusalem passed from the king of the south to the king of the north.

> *He will set his face to come with the power of his whole kingdom, bringing with him a proposal of peace which he will put into effect; he will also give him the daughter of women to ruin it. But she will not take a stand for him or be on his side.* —Daniel 11:17 NASB

In order to focus on the home front, Ptolemy signed a treaty with Antiochus III in 195 B.C., leaving the Seleucid king in possession of Coele-Syria. In order to establish some measure of control in Egypt and expand his empire, Antiochus III offered his daughter Cleopatra I in marriage to Ptolemy V (193–192 B.C.).[38] Unfortunately for Antiochus III, Cleopatra I was devoted to her husband, Ptolemy V, and stood by him rather than helping her father. At that time, Ptolemy V was about sixteen years old and Cleopatra I about ten years old. They had three children.[39] Clearly, Antiochus III did not think a young girl's heart could be turned to her husband alone.

4. Read Daniel 11:18. The king of the north sets his mind toward the coastal cities. What happens?

> *Then he will turn his face to the coastlands and capture many. But a commander will put a stop to his scorn against him; moreover, he will repay him for his scorn.* —Daniel 11:18 NASB

Greed for more land and control of the region seemed to be the driving force behind Antiochus III and he set his sights to secure the coastal towns that belonged to the remnants of the Ptolemaic dynasty. In 192 B.C., Antiochus III invaded Greece with a 10,000-man army and incurred the wrath of the Romans, who eventually defeated him at the Battle of Magnesia in 190 B.C.[40] This victory resulted in Roman domination over the internal affairs of a large part of the territory once controlled by the Seleucid Empire.

Wikipedia states the following:

> *The treaty forced upon Antiochus III by the victorious Romans was crippling, in the Treaty of Apamea Antiochus was forced to pay a huge war indemnity of 15,000 Talents along with giving up significant territory in Asia Minor. The Taurus Mountains became the new frontier. The Seleucid navy was limited by the treaty, and their squadrons of war elephants destroyed. It weakened the already fractious Seleucid Empire and halted all ambitions of Antiochus III of becoming a latter day Alexander in his own right. Polybius states the financial burden of war indemnity forced Antiochus III to loot Temple treasuries. This alienated Seleucid subjects and further reduced the dynasty's prestige, which had already been sharply reduced by the decisive defeat suffered against the Romans.[41]*

Antiochus III's all-consuming ambition to be like Alexander the Great, his predecessor, cost him everything, and then he made one more mistake.

> *So he will turn his face toward the fortresses of his own land, but he will stumble and fall and be found no more.* —Daniel 11:19 NASB

With the outlying provinces of the Seleucid Empire reasserting their independence from Antiochus III, his kingdom was now reduced to Syria, Mesopotamia, and Western Iran. Desperate to regain control of those areas, he mounted another expedition where he was murdered while pillaging a Temple of Bel at Elymaïs, Persia, in 187 B.C.[42] Some sources say he was plundering the Temple because he ran out of money that he needed to pay off Rome.

So far, history and the Bible have proven once again that the kings of the north and south are in our past. We will stop here today and continue with part three of the kings of the north and south in our next lesson.

LIFE APPLICATION: Pride, greed, and a complete lack of morals seem to be guiding both the king of the north and the king of the south. Even today, those who rule over us—presidents or prime ministers—often seem to operate in the same manner. Yet the Bible says there is no government anywhere that God has not placed in power (Romans 13:1). Reflect on that today because even though some governments are evil, they (like the kings of the north and south) are still part of God's plan to establish His kingdom on earth. While things may look bad now, remember they are that way in order to fulfill God's greater plan. Jesus is coming soon!

20. KINGS OF THE NORTH AND SOUTH (PART 3)

By now you are probably wondering how the kings of the north and south came to be regarded by theologians as "end-times" or future kings. Quite honestly, I have been wondering that myself. But we are not finished the book of Daniel yet and we may still discover that they are in our future.

Group Discussion:

So far, historical fact has proven the prophecy of the kings of the north and south has already been fulfilled. Yet end-time prophecy teachers keep insisting the kings of the north and south are still in our future. What is your opinion? Are we still looking at future events?

Read Daniel 11:20-30 and answer the following questions:

1. After Antiochus III, the king of the north, died, another rose in his place. What did he do and what were the results of his actions?

2. Another person (Daniel 11:21) arises and seizes the kingdom. How does he do it?

3. After an alliance is made, how does the king of the north act (Daniel 11:23)?

4. How does he gain the trust of the people (Daniel 11:24)?

5. Once again the king of the north proves his strength and the king of the south goes after him with a large army. Who wins (Daniel 11:25)?

6. What is at the heart of both kings? What is their intent (Daniel 11:27)?

7. Who else does the king of the north come against before he returns to his own land (Daniel 11:28)?

8. Who does the king of the north show regard for (Daniel 11:30)?

"There shall arise in his place one who imposes taxes on the glorious kingdom; but within a few days he shall be destroyed, but not in anger or in battle." —Daniel 11:20 NKJV

Seleucus IV Philopator took over after Antiochus III died. However, because of the heavy war indemnity exacted by Rome, he was forced to impose heavy taxes on his small empire. So he sent his minister Heliodorus to Jerusalem to seize the Jewish Temple treasury. You can read about it in 2 Maccabees 3:1-40. When Heliodorus returned from Jerusalem, he assassinated Seleucus IV Philopator and seized the throne for himself, under the pretense of being a co-regent for Seleucus' infant son (also named Antiochus).[43]

[21]And in his place shall arise a vile person, to whom they will not give the honor of royalty; but he shall come in peaceably, and seize the kingdom by intrigue. [22]With the force of a flood they shall be swept away from before him and be broken, and also the prince of the covenant. —Daniel 11:21-22 NKJV

The true heir to the throne, Demetrius, had previously been sent to Rome as a hostage under a hostage trade agreement. So the kingdom was seized from Heliodorus by Seleucus' younger brother, Antiochus Epiphanes IV. He acted as co-regent for his nephew, but in the end, murdered both Heliodorus and the young heir to the throne.

The prince of the covenant spoken of above is in reference to the High priest, Onias III, who was assassinated and deeply mourned by the Jewish people. It is his death that is spoken of in Daniel 8:9-11; Daniel 9:26; and of course, Daniel 11:22. He was regarded as a very pious man who opposed the Hellenization of the Temple. His death set the stage for complete Hellenization of the Temple and the eventual Maccabean revolt.

> [23] *After an alliance is made with him he will practice deception, and he will go up and gain power with a small force of people.* [24] *In a time of tranquility he will enter the richest parts of the realm, and he will accomplish what his fathers never did, nor his ancestors; he will distribute plunder, booty and possessions among them, and he will devise his schemes against strongholds, but only for a time.* —Daniel 11:23-24 NASB

While many claim the above verses are a prophecy yet to be fulfilled, it is clear from history that it already happened. Antiochus Epiphanes IV was a deceitful man. He must have been a very smooth talker as well because he did something his fathers never did. He was able to enter Egypt peaceably. He became co-regent for the king of the south, Ptolemy VI Philometer, who was about fourteen years of age and who just happened to be his nephew. He did this in response to an attack made on him by the young king's advisers at the time. When the Egyptians realized their folly in attacking Antiochus Epiphanes IV, they sent a delegation to negotiate a peace treaty. It was then that Antiochus took Ptolemy VI under his guardianship, resulting in Antiochus having some control over Egypt.[44]

As the Bible says, he practised deception. He did this by distributing the spoils he collected through war, sharing his bounty with the public. First Maccabees 3:30 hints at this. There are some reports that he would go into the streets and throw money at the citizens to gain their favour.

> [25] *He will stir up his strength and courage against the King of the South with a large army; so the King of the South will mobilize an extremely large and mighty army for war; but he will not stand, for schemes will be devised against him.* [26] *Those who eat his choice food will destroy him, and his army*

will overflow, but many will fall down slain. [27] As for both kings, their hearts will be intent on evil, and they will speak lies to each other at the same table; but it will not succeed, for the end is still to come at the appointed time. — Daniel 11:25-27 NASB

Unfortunately for him, Antiochus Epiphanes IV had not gained control of the city of Alexandria, and the people in that city were not happy with the influence Antiochus had over their young king. They responded by making Ptolemy VII, Philometer's younger brother, king. In response, Antiochus besieged Alexandria, but he was unable to cut communications to the city. So, at the end of 169 B.C., he withdrew his army. Instead of taking up arms against each other, the brothers decided to co-rule Egypt. This, of course, angered Antiochus, who invaded again. He seized Cyprus and Memphis. While at Memphis, Ptolemy VI Philometer and Antiochus had several meetings, each professing their allegiance to the other. Antiochus would profess he simply had the young king's interests at heart and Ptolemy VI would respond by saying how grateful he was to his uncle for taking an interest in his affairs. In reality, Ptolemy VI was smoothing things over with his brother Ptolemy VII so they could join forces against their deceitful uncle. Once again, Antiochus was marching on Alexandria when, on the outskirts of the capital, he met Popilius Laenas, who offered him an ultimatum from the Roman Senate: evacuate Egypt and Cyprus immediately or go up against the full force of Rome, who would send their entire fleet of ships from Kittim to come against him. Antiochus chose to withdraw, which ended the Sixth Syrian War and any further hope he had of conquering Egyptian territory.[45]

*[28] Then he will return to his land with much plunder; but his heart will be set against the holy covenant, and he will take action and then return to his own land. At the appointed time he will return and come into the South, but this last time it will not turn out the way it did before. [30] **For ships of Kittim***

will come against him; therefore he will be disheartened and will return and become enraged at the holy covenant and take action; so he will come back and show regard for those who forsake the holy covenant. —Daniel 11:28-30 NASB (emphasis mine)

Jason was the brother to the high priest Onias III, who was assassinated because of an ongoing dispute he had with Simon (a Hellenized Temple official and a member of the tribe of Benjamin). Onias was determined to keep to the laws of God and refused to give into those who wished to run the Temple according to Antiochus' wishes (making it Hellenized) rather than obeying God's laws. When he was assassinated, Jason became the new high priest. However, his time as high priest didn't last long. In 172 B.C., he sent Menelaus, Simon's brother, to deliver money to Antiochus Epiphanes IV. Menelaus used the opportunity to bribe Antiochus for the priesthood. He was successful and Antiochus confirmed Menelaus as the new high priest. As a result, Jason was forced to flee Jerusalem, but he found refuge in the land of the Ammonites.[46]

It was during this time that a rumour began regarding Antiochus IV's death. So Jason gathered a force of 1,000 soldiers and made a surprise attack on the city of Jerusalem. Menelaus was forced to flee Jerusalem, and when Antiochus returned from Egypt in 167 B.C., he attacked Jerusalem, restored Menelaus, and then executed many Jews.

[11]*When news of what had happened reached the king, he took it to mean that Judea was in revolt. So, raging inwardly, he left Egypt and took the city by storm.* [12] *He commanded his soldiers to cut down relentlessly everyone they met and to kill those who went into their houses.* [13]*Then there was a massacre of young and old, destruction of boys, women, and children, and slaughter of young girls and infants.* [14]*Within the total of three days eighty thousand were destroyed, forty thousand in hand-to-hand fighting, and as many were sold into slavery as were killed.* —2 Maccabees 5:11-14 NRSV

Not satisfied with that, Antiochus IV went into the Temple, guided by the Hellenized Menelaus, stole from the treasury, and then returned to Antioch, leaving governors to oppress the Jewish people. Only those Hellenized Jews who sided with Antiochus were left unharmed.

Antiochus' wrath against the Jews was brought on by his humiliating defeat by Egypt through Rome. So what many have perceived to be a future Antichrist was actually fulfilled in Antiochus Epiphanes IV. However, could a future Antichrist still be coming? We'll find out in our next lesson.

LIFE APPLICATION: Today, reflect on all you've learned. Compare it with commentaries that promote end-time kings of the north and south and see if it is lacking. Ask the Lord to reveal the truth to you. I've given you the facts. Now it's up to you to dig deeper for the truth.

21. KINGS OF THE NORTH AND SOUTH (PART 4)

So far we have seen history confirm that the kings of the north and south are not in our future but in our past. Today, we will finish our look at these kings to determine if anything at all concerning them is in our future. We will cover a lot of history. So pour a nice cup of coffee or tea and get settled in for some reading. But first, get out your Bible and answer the questions below.

Group Discussion:

Jesus warned in Matthew 24:15 that the "abomination of desolation" would happen again. We know it did (several times) and it may still be in our future if the third Temple gets built. Do you believe the kings of the north and south are in our future? Why or why not?

Read Daniel 11:31-45 and answer the following questions:

After his defeat in Egypt, the king of the north (Antiochus Epiphanes IV) returns to Jerusalem and he is angry. Scripture says "... he will come back and show regard for those who forsake the holy covenant" (Daniel 11:30). History shows Antiochus ordered his governors to show regard to those Jews who were Hellenized and willing to disregard the Temple rules of worship and sacrifice. Scripture verifies this in Daniel 11:31.

1. What do they do to the sanctuary and what happens to the sacrifice?

2. What do they set up in the Temple?

3. How does he convince people to act wickedly towards the Jews?

4. What do the faithful do in response?

5. What happens to those who go up against the king of the north?

6. A new king arises, beginning in Daniel 11:36. How does this king exalt himself and how long does this indignation last?

7. Daniel 11:38 says the king will honour a god of fortresses. How does he do that?

8. What does this king do for those who acknowledge him?

9. The king of the south attacks this new king and the king of the north comes against him as well. Which countries are rescued out of his hand?

10. The land of Egypt does not escape from this king. What does he gain from them (Daniel 11:42-43)?

11. Who else follows this king (Daniel 11:43)?

12. Rumours from the east and north disturb the king. What does he do?

13. What happens to the king in the end?

Do these final verses of Daniel 11 depict a future Antichrist and wars between the kings of the north and south? Let's find out by comparing scripture to history one last time.

I won't go into details again about Antiochus Epiphanes IV and his desecration of the Temple in Jerusalem and what he did to the Jews. For review you may turn back to chapter twelve. Suffice it to say that from Daniel 11:22-35, the king of the north was Antiochus Epiphanes IV and he did everything Daniel said he would do. After venting his anger on the Jews and on their Temple (abomination of desolation), he then decreed that his entire kingdom should worship one god and become one people, each giving up their own customs in favour of unity. Through his smooth words, he was able to convince everyone but the non-Hellenized Jews. All the laws of God were forbidden. The Torah was outlawed, as was circumcision and the Jews faced death if they dared to celebrate the Sabbaths, or any feasts or if they were caught praying. Yet, faithful Jews remained strong and stood firm against Antiochus.

> [34]*Now when they fall they will be granted a little help, and many will join with them in hypocrisy.* [35]*Some of those who have insight will fall, in order to refine, purge and make them pure until the end time; because it is still to come at the appointed time.* —Daniel 11:34-35 NASB

The verse above speaks of the Maccabean revolt. I highly recommend you read the first and second books of the Maccabees. These are considered historical documents rather than scripture. You can find them online at www.Biblegateway.com, under the Anglican or Catholic versions of the Bible. These books give a detailed account of what happened between the Jews and Antiochus. It began with a priest (Mattathias) who served in the Temple. When he refused to sacrifice a pig on the altar, another Jewish priest stepped forward to do it. In righteous anger and indignation, Mattathias killed the priest and then slew the government official who was making them perform these sacrifices. After which he said in 1 Maccabees 2:27, "Let everyone who has zeal for the Torah and who stands by the covenant follow me!" Thus began the Maccabean revolt and the beginning of Hasmonean rule in Judea.

Mattathias was a son of Yohannan, grandson of Simeon, a Hasmonean. An edict was issued for his arrest because of the murders in the Temple, but Mattathias had escaped to the wilderness of Judea with his five sons—Judah, Eleazar, Simon, John, and Jonathan—and called upon all Jews to follow him. Many responded to his call. Some, as the verse above suggests, "joined them in hypocrisy."

This was an important step for the Jews as it was the first time in 400 years they had asserted their independence. Mattathias' sons Judah, Simon, and Jonathan began a military campaign that had disastrous results. Because these were Jews who followed God's laws, they would not fight on the Sabbath. Thus, 1,000 Jewish men, women, and children were killed by Seleucid troops because they refused to fight even in self-defense. After that, it was decided self-defense was a valid reason to fight on the Sabbath. On the 25th of Kislev 164 B.C., Jerusalem was recaptured by the Jews and the Temple was cleansed. Antiochus died later that year and Demetrius (the nephew whose throne he had usurped) finally took the throne. The history from here is far too involved and too long to go into, but suffice it to say that during numerous wars to retake Jerusalem, Hasmonean rule lasted from Mattathias' leadership in 168 B.C. to 37 B.C., when King Herod, who came to power under the Romans, around 48 B.C., ended their reign. Daniel 11:35 suggests the end of Hasmonean rule:

Some of those who have insight will fall, in order to refine, purge and make them pure until the end time; because it is still to come at the appointed time.

Between the writings of Josephus Flavius, the books of the Maccabees, and Daniel himself, it is quite clear that Antiochus Epiphanes IV fulfills what many evangelical Christians believe to be a description of the future Antichrist or "king of the north."

You may be asking if anything we've studied so far in the book of Daniel speaks about Jesus. Yes, of course. Remember Daniel's dream of the four beasts in chapter seven? So far we have discovered all four of those beasts were fulfilled through various governments (Babylonian, Persian, Greek, and Roman) and as Daniel 2:44 predicted, would bring us to the very beginning of Jesus' life. Starting with Daniel 11:36, a new king emerges who would feel threatened by Jesus and he was just as awful as Antiochus Epiphanes IV.

[36]Then the king will do as he pleases, and he will exalt and magnify himself above every god and will speak monstrous things against the God of gods; and he will prosper until the indignation is finished, for that which is decreed will be done. [37] He will show no regard for the gods of his fathers or for the desire of women, nor will he show regard for any other god; for he will magnify himself above them all. —Daniel 11:36-37 NASB

After Antiochus' death, his empire began to disintegrate, largely due to the Maccabean revolt and the rise of Hasmonean rule. By 100 B.C. the once formidable Seleucid Empire encompassed little more than Antioch and some Syrian cities.[47] This, of course, set the stage for the rise of the Roman Empire.

After the Roman conquest of Pontus, the Romans became alarmed at the constant source of instability in Syria under the Seleucids. If you read about the kings after Antiochus Epiphanes IV and realize the drama and instability in their own households (lots of murdering, poisoning, and usurping of thrones), it is easy to see why the Seleucid Empire began to crumble. They made it far too easy for Rome to come in and get rid of them entirely. In 63 B.C., Pompey saw the Seleucids as too troublesome to continue. So he made Syria into a Roman province and did away with any remaining princes.[48] But Syria was the capital of the king of the north and the Bible indicates he will rise again in one form or another. Remember that as we continue.

But now the prophecy shifts to a different king. How do we know it is a different king? Verse thirty-seven says, "He will show no regard for the gods of his fathers." If Antiochus Epiphanes IV was anything, he was zealous that people (all people) worship Zeus (the god of his fathers) in unity.

So what other king who ruled over Jerusalem exalted himself like Antiochus?

It is at this point that most scholars insist we are looking at an end-time Antichrist. Many believe, due to current events, that we are living in those days and that the "new king" is represented by Islam and the rise of an Islamic Caliphate, largely because of war-torn Syria, where the king of the north came from. However, as history shows, another king rose to prominence in Judea who acted like Antiochus and put an end to Hasmonean rule as Daniel 11:35 predicted. So let's look at this king and find out who he was in history.

[36]*"Then the king will do as he pleases, and he will exalt and magnify himself above every god and will speak monstrous things against the God of gods; and he will prosper until the indignation is finished, for that which is decreed will be done. [37]He will show no regard for the gods of his fathers or for the desire of women, nor will he show regard for any other god; for he will magnify himself above them all. [38] But instead he will honor a god of fortresses, a god whom his fathers did not know; he will honor him with gold, silver, costly stones and treasures. [39]He will take action against the strongest of fortresses with the help of a foreign god; he will give great honor to those who acknowledge him and will cause them to rule over the many, and will parcel out land for a price."*—Daniel 11:36-39 NASB*

One king appeared in history toward the end of Hasmonean rule who fulfilled all the prophetic verses above. That king was Herod, the same King Herod who was reigning when Jesus was born. Let's look at his life and see if he fulfilled the verses above.

Did Herod do as he pleased? Did he exalt and magnify himself above God and speak monstrous things about Him?

Herod was an Arab of Edomite descent whose ancestors had converted to Judaism under Hasmonean rule. He has been described as "a madman who murdered his own family and a great many rabbis," "the evil genius of the Judean nation," "prepared to commit any crime in order to gratify his unbounded ambition," and "the greatest builder in Jewish history."[49] Antipater, Herod's father, appointed Herod governor of Galilee at 25 years of age.

Herod enjoyed the backing of Rome and was soon appointed King of the Jews by the Roman Senate. His appointment would bring an end to Hasmonean rule and the capture of Jerusalem. Did he do as he pleased? Yes, his tyrannical rule is well-documented in Josephus Flavius' *Jewish Antiquities*. Worried about his throne, he executed several members of his family, including his wife and sons. He murdered those from the Hasmonean line who might be a threat to his throne. He was the reason Jewish (Hasmonean) rule ended and Roman occupation began. And yet, despite his dubious background, he claimed he was a Jew and magnified himself above God by calling himself the King of the Jews.

His decadent lifestyle often put him at odds with the Sanhedrin and Jewish and non-Jewish people in general. He heavily taxed the people he governed in order to pay for his lavish building projects. As for respecting Jewish law, he had a golden eagle erected at the entrance of the Temple, which repulsed Jewish leaders who regarded it as an idol. Like Antiochus, he forced the Jews to participate in heathen games and even combat with wild animals.[50] He also built temples and idols for other religions outside Jerusalem. He had no regard for the gods of his fathers because he quite literally had no regard for any god at all. His religion was whatever benefited him the most. In other words, he cared more for himself than God, therefore exalting himself above God.

In addition to all that, in Matthew 2:16-18, Herod learned that the one true God had sent His Son, the real King of the Jews. When he realized he had been deceived by the Magi about Jesus' whereabouts, he ordered all infants under the age of two massacred. As far as Herod was concerned, he alone was king and no "god" would tell him otherwise.

He will show no regard for the gods of his fathers or for the desire of women, nor will he show regard for any other god; for he will magnify himself above them all. —Daniel 11:37 NASB

Some people have taken the above verse and construed it to mean that Herod was gay. While Herod no doubt led a decadent lifestyle, this verse has nothing to do with homosexuality. It clearly says he showed no regard for the gods of his fathers and no regard for the desire of women. In other words, he didn't care what they liked, wanted or desired.

The Hebrew word for desire is *chemdat* and it means "that which is desirable." It was the hope of every religious Jewish woman that she might be the mother of the prophesied Messiah. Therefore, it was primarily the Messiah who was "the desire" of Jewish women, and Herod, by defiantly murdering all male boys under the age of two, showed he had no regard for their desires. He also showed through this massacre that he knew the Scriptures. He knew a Saviour was coming (the King of the Jews) and he was convinced that by killing these babies, he could defeat God, thereby magnifying himself above the one true God.

Did Herod honour a god of fortresses?

But instead he will honor a god of fortresses, a god whom his fathers did not know; he will honor him with gold, silver, costly stones and treasures. [39] He will take action against the strongest of fortresses with the help of a foreign god; he will give great honor to those who acknowledge him and will cause them to rule over the many, and will parcel out land for a price. — Daniel 11:38-39 NASB

The phrase "god of fortresses"—or "god of forces"—in some Bibles is fascinating because it speaks of Herod's architectural accomplishments. His most famous and ambitious project was, of course, the Second Temple in Jerusalem. While construction had been completed on the Temple back when Darius the Great was king, Herod continued to add to it, making it more to his liking rather than to God's. I often wonder if this is why Jesus predicted it would be destroyed.

But Herod's other great accomplishments (and there were many) were the fortresses Masada, Antonia Fortress in Jerusalem, and Herodium to name a few. These architectural wonders speak quite clearly as to where Herod's worship was directed. Always catering to Rome, he built these lavish fortresses primarily for his own security and wealth but also to bring honour and glory to Rome (many were built in honour of Roman emperors and used in worship of those emperors), who benefitted from his building projects. So with the "help of a foreign god" (Rome), Herod was able to establish his kingdom. And as Daniel predicted, he even gave land to those who supported him in order to gain their allegiance. Josephus confirms this in his works *Jewish Antiquities XV 8:5.*

Did the kings of the south and north storm against him? Did he enter "the Beautiful Land"? Did many countries fall? Who escaped?

> [40]*And at the time of the end shall the King of the South push at him: and the King of the north shall come against him like a whirlwind, with chariots, and with horsemen, and with many ships; and he shall enter into the countries, and shall overflow and pass over.* [41] *He shall enter also into the glorious land, and many countries shall be overthrown: but these shall escape out of his hand, even Edom, and Moab, and the chief of the children of Ammon.* [42] *He shall stretch forth his hand also upon the countries: and the land of Egypt shall not escape.* [43] *But he shall have power over the treasures of gold and of silver, and over all the precious things of Egypt: and the Libyans and the Ethiopians shall be at his steps. —Daniel 11:40-43 KJV*

Even though Herod was granted the title "King of Judea" by the Roman senate, he still had to show his worthiness to the emperor, Caesar Augustus (Octavius). He was but a vassal of the Roman Empire and so their interests were his as well. Unfortunately, he made the mistake of showing his support for Marc Antony, Octavius's rival. Antony, the king of the south, (yes, he was the same one who loved Cleopatra) went to war against Octavius. Octavius was the official representative of Rome. He was also the ruler of the former Syrian empire of the Seleucids, which made him (by default) the king of the north. This war between Antony, a "new king" and Caesar Augustus finds its fulfillment in King Herod.

It was Marc Antony, at the urging of Cleopatra and with assistance from Herod, who first attacked the king of the north. But Octavius came against him exactly as Daniel predicted, "like a whirlwind, with chariots, horsemen and many ships," and soundly defeated Marc Antony. Herod, realizing his huge error in siding with Antony, went immediately to Octavius, concocting an incredible story about loyalty and how he would be as loyal to him as he had been to Antony. He then acknowledged Octavius as Caesar Augustus, supreme ruler of Rome. Octavius accepted Herod's pledge and promised him continued rule over Judea.[51]

> [41]*"He shall also enter the Glorious Land, and many countries shall be overthrown; but these shall escape from his hand: Edom, Moab, and the prominent people of Ammon.* [42]*He shall stretch out his hand against the countries, and the land of Egypt shall not escape."* —Daniel 11:41-42 NKJV

Octavius did invade Egypt by way of the Glorious Land (aka Judea), at which time, Herod rendered him much assistance. Josephus says:

> *"Caesar went for Egypt through Syria when Herod received him with royal and rich entertainments; and then did he first of all ride along with Caesar, as he was reviewing his army about Ptolemais, and feasted him with all his friends, and then distributed among the rest of his army what was necessary to feast them withal."* —Wars I, 20, 3

So once again history played out as the Bible predicted. The reference in Daniel 11:41 to the countries of Edom, Moab, and Ammon (Edom, Moab, and the children of Ammon are modern day Jordan) had a geographical significance to Daniel and to others of his day, who knew them to be the people of the lands adjacent to Judea on the east and south. It is recorded in history that those countries *did* escape from the hand of Augustus. This is in strong contrast with the next verse, which says: "And the land of Egypt *shall not escape*" (Daniel 11:42). Marc Antony, realizing he had no way of escape, committed suicide and fell on his own sword, and we all know how his co-conspirator, Cleopatra, died, from the bite of an asp.

He shall have power over the treasures of gold and silver, and over all the precious things of Egypt; also the Libyans and Ethiopians shall follow at his heels. —Daniel 11:43 NKJV

In the days of Antony and Cleopatra, the riches of Egypt were vast. When Herod helped Caesar Augustus during the invasion of Egypt, he was given land by Augustus that stretched his kingdom from Syria all the way to parts of Egypt, thereby taking Rome from a Republic and turning it into an Empire. While these verses do speak mainly of the king of the north's conquests, it was with the help of Herod that Augustus was able to enlarge his kingdom. With the conquest of Egypt and Libya, Libyans and Ethiopians realized the strength of Herod and Rome and as the Scriptures suggest, "followed at his heels."

But news from the east and the north shall trouble him; therefore he shall go out with great fury to destroy and annihilate many. —Daniel 11:44 NKJV

Now at last we come to that point in time when Jesus makes His appearance. It is prophesied in the verse above and comes to fruition in Matthew 2:1-12, when wise men from the east came seeking information about the King of the Jews.

[1]Now when Jesus was born in Bethlehem of Judaea in the days of Herod the king, behold, there came wise men from the east to Jerusalem, [2]saying, Where is he that is born King of the Jews? For we have seen his star in the

east, and are come to worship him. ³When Herod the king had heard these things, he was troubled, and all Jerusalem with him. —Matthew 2:1-3 KJV

And we know what Herod did when he heard this troubling news that threatened his throne:

Then Herod, when he saw that he was deceived by the wise men, was exceedingly angry; and he sent forth and put to death all the male children who were in Bethlehem and in all its districts, from two years old and under, according to the time which he had determined from the wise men. — Matthew 2:16 NKJV

As Daniel 11:44 says, he "annihilated many." And what was the news from the north that troubled him? Antipater, his oldest son, who lived in Rome, sent letters to his father. In these letters he revealed that two of his brothers, whom Herod meant to make his successors, had denigrated their father to Caesar. These "tidings out of the north" troubled Herod so much that he had his two sons killed. Then later, Antipater himself was executed for his conspiracy in the matter. This caused Herod again to break forth with intense fury against his own sons, as related by Josephus at great length in *Jewish Antiquities* XVII 4-7 and *Wars* 1:30-33.

However, his fury was not spent and after killing the Jewish children in Bethlehem and then his own sons, he burned alive those who had pulled down his golden image of the Roman eagle from the gate of the Temple.

And he shall plant the tents of his palace between the seas and the glorious holy mountain; yet he shall come to his end, and no one will help him. — Daniel 11:45 NKJV

Herod had many palaces, and in March, 4 B.C., he retired to his winter palace at Jericho, less than ten miles northwest of the Dead Sea, about forty-five miles east of the Mediterranean Sea, and less than twenty miles northeast of Jerusalem. So he was between the seas and the glorious holy mountain and died a horrible death after a prolonged illness. Some believe from Josephus' description of his illness that he died of syphilis.

> *But now Herod's distemper greatly increased upon him after a severe manner, and this by God's judgment upon him for his sins; for a fire glowed in him slowly, which did not so much appear to the touch outwardly, as it augmented his pains inwardly; for it brought upon him a vehement appetite to eating, which he could not avoid to supply with one sort of food or other. His entrails were also ex-ulcerated, and the chief violence of his pain lay on his colon; an aqueous and transparent liquor also had settled itself about his feet, and a like matter afflicted him at the bottom of his belly. Nay, further, his privy-member was putrefied, and produced worms; and when he sat upright, he had a difficulty of breathing, which was very loathsome, on account of the stench of his breath, and the quickness of its returns; he had also convulsions in all parts of his body, which increased his strength to an insufferable degree. It was said by those who pretended to divine, and who were endued with wisdom to foretell such things, that God inflicted this punishment on the king on account of his great impiety; yet was he still in hopes of recovering, though his afflictions seemed greater than anyone could bear* (Josephus Flavius, *Jewish Antiquities*, Book 17, Ch. 6:5).

Clearly, the references to the kings of the north and south down to the final "new king" were all fulfilled in history. Nothing in Daniel 11 indicates a future king of the north or king of the south. So where does that leave us in regard to Daniel and end-time events? We still have one final chapter.

LIFE APPLICATION: Now that you have seen the book of Daniel play out in history, how does it make you feel? Are you comforted by the fact that God's plan took us right up to the time of Jesus' birth? Today, praise the Lord for His ways and His plans because they are always right and as we've seen, always have a purpose.

22. A LOOK INTO THE FUTURE?

At the beginning of our Daniel study, we were given a history of why Daniel and his people had been exiled. We got a look at King Nebuchadnezzar (the first beast) and we got a glimpse into the future kings (beasts) who would conquer him. In addition, we have learned that ten kingdoms/kings are still in our future. However, throughout the study we have seen that what most think of as future events have already happened and we have verified this through history. So where does that leave us—especially since chapter twelve gives us the hint of future events?

The beginning of Daniel 12 is a continuation of Daniel 11. In Daniel 11, an angel is sent to Daniel to explain to him what is going to happen to his people. The last line of Daniel 11 reads like this:

And he shall plant the tents of his palace between the seas and the glorious holy mountain; yet he shall come to his end, and no one will help him. — Daniel 11:45 NKJV

The "he" referred to is King Herod the Great. His death is foretold by the angel and now the angel continues with what will happen next. Keep this in mind when you read the first line of Daniel 12, which says:

"At that time Michael shall stand up, the great prince who stands watch over the sons of your people; and there shall be a time of trouble, such as never was since there was a nation, even to that time. And at that time your people shall be delivered, everyone who is found written in the book." — Daniel 12:1 NKJV

Group Discussion:

Daniel 12:1 got me excited. How about you? In this verse God reveals to Daniel that his people shall be delivered. But He goes a bit further and says, ". . . *everyone* who is found written in the book" (emphasis mine). How does it make you feel knowing that from the first chapter of Daniel to the last, God's plan (as horrible as it sounded) would include Jesus and redemption for you and me?

Read Daniel 12:1-13 and answer the following questions:

1. Keeping in mind that chapter twelve is a continuation of chapter eleven, when will the archangel Michael stand up?

2. Who does Michael stand watch over?

3. Who will be rescued at that time?

4. Will the dead rise? If so, what will happen to them?

5. Describe those who are wise or have insight (Daniel 12:3).

6. How long is Daniel to seal up his book?

7. While the book is sealed, what shall increase?

8. In Daniel 12:6, an angel asks, "How long will it be until the end of these wonders?" What was he told?

9. When the power of the holy people has been completely shattered, all these things shall be finished. Who are the holy people and what things is the angel referring to?

10. Who will not understand what is happening? Who will?

One of the things we need to remember when interpreting Daniel is that it was given for specific reasons to a specific people. So far, we have seen that almost all of Daniel has been fulfilled. Yet, the ten horns are still in our future, as discussed earlier. We have also seen throughout this study that Daniel encompasses the entire time from the Jewish captivity in Babylon to (as we will discover in this chapter) Jesus' time, the destruction of the Temple and Jerusalem in A.D. 70, and right up to the present day. So what do we know about Daniel so far?

Facts about the book of Daniel:

- It was written about the nation of Israel (Daniel 10:14; Daniel 9:14-27; Daniel 11:14; Daniel 12:1).
- It was written to reveal what would happen to the Jewish people during *their* latter days as a nation, from captivity to the destruction of Jerusalem and the Temple (Daniel 10:14).
- Almost all the events in Daniel have been fulfilled. Right up until the holy people (the Jewish nation) were

scattered by Rome in 70 A.D., with the destruction of the Temple and Jerusalem (Daniel 12:7). There is one exception: the ten horns mentioned in Daniel that come out of the Roman Empire.

- Each book of the Bible is consistent in its telling and they all have a purpose and theme. The book of Daniel's theme and purpose were to explain why the Jews were in captivity and what would happen to them in the future, with the prediction of four kingdoms coming to conquer the Jewish people. We know that this prophecy ends with the final kingdom, Rome.

- We know that during the fourth beast's reign (Rome), God set up a kingdom that shall never be destroyed. He did so by sending His Son Jesus Christ (Daniel 2:44).

- The prophecy of Daniel covers every important event that happened to the Jews, from their captivity to the coming of their Messiah to the destruction of Jerusalem and the Temple.

- With the exception of the ten horns mentioned in Daniel, which come out of the Roman Empire, everything else has been fulfilled.

Based on these facts, we must trust that the warning God intended for Daniel and his people was simply that, a warning of what was going to happen during the time period of the four beasts (Babylon, Persia, Greece, and Rome).

I do not believe it is coincidence that Jesus came before the destruction of Jerusalem and the Temple. His warning in Matthew 24, that great tribulation was coming (greater than that of Antiochus Epiphanes IV) was no coincidence. The fact that the Apostle John was given further revelation is even more reason to believe that Daniel is not a book specifically about the end-times so much as it is a book about the end of the nation of Israel at that time. So let's look at Daniel 12 verse by verse and find out once and for all if any of the prophecies in this book are in our future.

> **At that time** Michael shall stand up, the great prince who stands watch over the sons of your people. And there **shall be a time of trouble**; such as never was since there was a nation, **even to that time**. And **at that time** your people shall be delivered, everyone who is found written in the book. — Daniel 12:1 NKJV (emphasis mine)

What clues does the verse above give us in regard to its timing? The first three words, "at that time," show us the angel (who has been narrating) is referring to the last verse in Daniel 11. "At that time" refers to the time of the fourth beast (Rome) and in particular, King Herod and his successors. The archangel Michael, who stands guard or watches over the Jewish people, stands up (or is on alert). Why? Because a time of trouble since Israel became a nation was about to occur. Daniel 12:1 goes on to say that "at that time," Daniel's people would be delivered—but only those whose names were found written in the book (probably the Book of Life). Do not forget that the Book of Life is not exclusive to Christians. Many Old Testament heroes like Abraham, David, Moses, and others were saved through faith in God alone. However, since we know that Jesus came during the time of Jewish rebellion against the Romans, we have the promise of His death and resurrection fulfilling Daniel 12:1.

> And many of those who sleep in the dust of the earth shall awake, some to everlasting life, some to shame and everlasting contempt. —Daniel 12:2 NKJV

It would appear that this verse indicates a resurrection of the dead at the end of all time. But Daniel is not dealing with "end of time" theology but rather the latter days of the Jewish nation during Roman times up until the destruction of the second Temple and Jerusalem. Even Jews today do not consider Daniel to be in reference to any end-time or future events. To them, the book of Daniel confirms their history up until the time of the destruction of the Temple. So what could the verse above possibly mean? There are two possibilities. First, when John the Baptist and Jesus appeared on the scene, they came upon a nation in slumber (Isaiah 29:9-10). It was a nation that was ignorant and worldly, who had forgotten why they had fought Antiochus Epiphanes IV. So when John appeared—this "voice crying out in the wilderness to repent"—they were jarred into remembering the prophets of old. It had been about 400 years since they had heard a prophet speak on behalf of God. Then Jesus appeared and the whole world at that time was turned upside down by this unassuming Jew from Galilee. To say some woke to everlasting life and some to shame and everlasting contempt could be a metaphor on how the people at that time responded to Jesus. Some accepted him as their Messiah, those who did not called for his execution. In other words, some woke up to the truth their Messiah had appeared, while others stayed asleep in their ignorance. However, when the angel says, "Many of those who sleep in the dust of the earth shall awake," it could be in reference to what happened after Jesus died on the cross.

[52] The tombs were opened, and many bodies of the saints who had fallen asleep were raised; [53] and coming out of the tombs after His resurrection they entered the holy city and appeared to many. —Matthew 27:52-53 NASB

So while Daniel does not speak specifically about Jesus, it does take us to His time and fulfills New Testament accounts.

Those who have insight will shine brightly like the brightness of the expanse of heaven, and those who lead the many to righteousness, like the stars forever and ever. —Daniel 12:3 NASB

The above verse could be in reference to Jesus' followers. Scripture confirms that thousands were coming to Christ every day as the apostles boldly proclaimed Jesus as Messiah. Acts 2:41 confirms that more than 3,000 people came to Christ in one day at the time of Pentecost.

But you, Daniel, shut up the words, and seal the book until the time of the end; many shall run to and fro, and knowledge shall increase. —Daniel 12:4 NKJV

Many Bible translations read "seal the book until the end of time," making this jump from a book about Daniel and his people to a book about the end of the world. The NKJV translates this as "until the time of the end," meaning the end of Israel as a nation, not the end of the world. Daniel is told to "shut up the words," or in other words, close the book, as the prophecy stops here. The angel assures Daniel that as the years pass, many people will come and go and their knowledge will increase as Daniel's prophesies unfold before their eyes. Knowledge did increase when Jesus commissioned His disciples to "go into all the world and preach the gospel to all creation" (Mark 16:15). Daniel's prophecy, therefore, unfolded before the eyes of the people of Jesus' day and they came awake to the reality that God was at work in their midst. The same thing is happening to us as we see the events of Revelation unfolding before our eyes that signal the return of Jesus.

The book of Daniel, therefore, is a prophecy for the nation of Israel, whereas the book of Revelation is a prophecy for the entire world.

[5]Then I, Daniel, looked; and there stood two others, one on this riverbank and the other on that riverbank. [6]And one said to the man clothed in linen, who was above the waters of the river, "How long shall the fulfillment of these wonders be?"

[7]Then I heard the man clothed in linen, who was above the waters of the river, when he held up his right hand and his left hand to heaven, and swore by Him who lives forever, that it shall be for a time, times, and half a time;

and when the power of the holy people has been completely shattered, all these things shall be finished. —Daniel 12:5-7 NKJV

Daniel asks this question: "How long shall the fulfillment of these wonders be?" In no uncertain terms, the man clothed in linen lets Daniel know that "it shall be for a time, times, and half a time; and *when the power of the holy people has been completely shattered, all these things shall be finished.*" So Daniel gets two clues. One is sort of confusing and the other is that his people will be completely shattered after all these things come to pass.

We'll deal with the second part first. In A.D. 63, when the Romans conquered Jerusalem, the former Hasmonean Dynasty (the nation of Israel) became a protectorate of Rome. In other words, if they were attacked by another nation, they would be "protected" by Rome. However, in order to keep this protection, Rome taxed the Jews to the breaking point, and equally infuriating, they took over the appointment of the high priest. As a result, the high priests, who represented the Jews before God, increasingly came from the ranks of Jews who collaborated with Rome. Thus, the high priests who stepped into the Holy of Holies once a year and offered daily sacrifices were becoming more and more corrupt. When Jesus cleansed the Temple (Matthew 21:13; Mark 11:17; Luke 19:46), He knew how desperate the situation had become, for He had seen their hypocrisy.

In A.D. 66, the last Roman procurator, Florus, stole a large sum of silver from the Temple. This action, combined with years of heavy taxation and abuses by Rome, led to the Jewish people finally revolting against Rome. This revolt was fueled by a group called the Zealots. The Jews were so outraged over the actions of Florus they wiped out the small Roman garrison that was stationed in Jerusalem. After Cestius Gallus, the Roman ruler in neighbouring Syria, sent in reinforcements, the Jews routed them too.[52]

Encouraged by this victory, many Jews naively believed they could defeat Rome. This belief was fueled by the Zealots and their ranks grew. Soon they would take over the now famous fortress of Masada, where they held out for three years before committing mass suicide.

The Romans launched their first attack in the most radicalized area, Galilee. They had over 60,000 heavily armed and professional troops. The results were disastrous and an estimated 100,000 Jews were killed or sold into slavery.

Those refugees who escaped the Galilean massacre then made their way to Jerusalem. For three and a half years (1,290 days), they fought, and in the end, it is estimated that as many as one million Jews died in the Great Revolt against Rome.[53] The day the Temple was destroyed was the day the daily sacrifice was taken away. In the end, just as the book of Daniel predicted, the Jewish people were shattered and it led to a total loss of Jewish political authority in Israel until 1948, when the Jewish people became a nation once again.

The entire prophecy of Daniel comes to a close with the scattering of the Jewish people. Jesus warned His disciples that such a scattering would occur:

And they will fall by the edge of the sword, and be led away captive into all nations. And Jerusalem will be trampled by Gentiles until the times of the Gentiles are fulfilled. —Luke 21:24 NKJV

Now for the confusing part of Daniel 12:5-7. Twice in Daniel and once in Revelation we see the phrase "time, times, and half a time." So what does it all mean? Are they related in anyway?

In both Daniel and Revelation, we are given the exact number of days that show us how long this fixed time period will be. Revelation 12:6 gives us the number 1,260 days. While Daniel 12:11 gives us 1,290 days. So we know immediately the two are not related. "Days" in Greek is *hēmera* and means "the day," or the interval between sunrise and sunset. "Days" in

Hebrew is *yowm* and also means "day," or a twenty-four hour period. When we divide 1,260 by 360 days (a year, according to the Hebrew calendar), we get 3.5 years. In Daniel the time is a little longer at 3.58 years.

So when the angel says to Daniel, *"From the time that the daily sacrifice is taken away, and the abomination of desolation is set up, there shall be one thousand two hundred and ninety days,"* he is letting Daniel know there will be another occasion when an abomination will happen in the Temple.

In A.D. 70, this happened when the Temple Mount was invaded by Roman soldiers who set fire to the Holy of Holies and slaughtered those Jews who tried to stop them. It is not about our future and an Antichrist who will make a peace covenant with Israel then break it midway. The book of Daniel is a prophecy that is about one thing: the history of the Jewish nation from the time of their captivity in Babylon to the appearance of their Messiah to the destruction of the Temple in A.D. 70. Then the book is closed and the prophecy ends.

"But you, go your way till the end; for you shall rest, and will arise to your inheritance at the end of the days."—Daniel 12:13 NKJV

In the end, Daniel is promised that he will rise at the end of days, during the resurrection. He would live to see the fall of Nebuchadnezzar and the invasion of the Persian Empire.

So now we have come to the end of our study. We have seen that the book of Daniel is a book for the Jewish people alone, dealing specifically with their history. Yet within its pages, we see the prediction of the Messiah and the promise of a kingdom that will never be destroyed. Scripture reminds us, however, that God is not finished with Israel—nor are her enemies. We also learned of a coming ten-nation (ten horns) alliance, which will come from the Roman Empire and be instrumental in end-time events that are predicted in the book of Revelation. For we know in the last days that all nations will come against Israel and the Lord has said He will destroy them all (Zechariah 12:9).

One thing we can be certain of: Jesus is coming again, and just as the Jews had the book of Daniel as a warning, we have the book of Revelation to show us what to expect in these final days. The next book in the Digging Deeper series will be on Revelation, so if you wish to be notified when it becomes available sign up to my email list at www.laurajdavis.com.

Thank you for journeying with me through this study. I hope it has encouraged you and enlightened you. May God bless you as you continue to study His Word, digging deeper into His truths, so that you may grow in your walk with Him.

LIFE APPLICATION: You have discovered over the last few lessons that most of Daniel's prophecy has already been fulfilled, according to history. Therefore, today would be a good day to get out your commentaries on Daniel or search online to find out why today's prophecy teachers insist it is in our future. I have presented you with history and the Scriptures. Now it's your job to dig deeper to discover these truths for yourself.

FACILITATOR'S GUIDE AND ANSWER KEY

If you are studying *Unlocking the Truth of Daniel* in a group setting, it is always best to appoint a leader or facilitator. I like the term facilitator because the word leader puts too much pressure on the individual to have all the answers. And that is not how a group Bible study should be run. A group study should allow all participants the chance to share:

- What they personally learned during their study times throughout the week.
- Questions without fear of reproach.
- What troubled them about the study (i.e. difficulties in grasping concepts presented).
- Insights they gleaned that the study might not have touched on.

If you are the facilitator of your group, your main job will be to keep everyone on time and on track. Not every question needs to be addressed at each meeting. Some may prove more time-consuming than others. It is up to the facilitator to decide when to move on because if you don't, a Bible study that would normally take one hour could easily stretch into two hours, leaving you little time for prayer or fellowship afterwards.

Begin and end each meeting with prayer, inviting the Holy Spirit to lead the participants into all truth. Make sure to read the material beforehand. Keep a highlighter handy as it helps to highlight those areas you think will need to be discussed. As you get further into the study, you will find this practice very helpful, as the concepts and history that are presented may be unfamiliar to participants. Let the Spirit lead you. You do not have to touch on each question. Use the answer key below when you find yourself stumped.

If you are doing this study alone, pray first and ask the Holy Spirit to open your eyes to understand God's Word. Take your time and go at your own pace. Use the answer key as a last resort if you are stumped. Let the Holy Spirit guide you into all truth.

May God bless you as you dig into His Word!

Answer Key

I use the NKJV or the NASB. If you do not have one of those translations and you find yourself stumped on a question, visit www.Biblegateway.com, where they have many translations to choose from.

Chapter One: Standing Firm

Read Daniel 1:1-21.

1. The events of this chapter occur in the third year of the reign of Jehoiakim, king of Judah (605 B.C.).
2. Nebuchadnezzar was the king of Babylon and he came to Jerusalem and besieged it.
3. Nebuchadnezzar captured all the officers and fighting men. All the skilled workers and artisans were captured, a total of 10,000 men. Also captured were Jehoiakim, king of Judah; his mother; his attendants; his nobles; and his officials. Nebuchadnezzar also took 7,000 men of valour, and 1,000 craftsmen and smiths, who were strong and fit for war.
4. Only the poorest people of the land were left behind.
5. He carried all the articles from the Temple of God, both large and small, the treasures of the Lord's Temple, and the treasures of the king and his officials to Babylon.

6. Nebuchadnezzar took his captives into the land of Shinar (Babylon).

7. He brought the vessels into the treasure house of his god.

8. They had to be young men in whom there was no blemish. They were to be good-looking, gifted in all wisdom, possessing knowledge, and quick to understand, those who had the ability to serve in the king's palace.

9. The king ordered Ashpenaz to teach them the language and literature of the Chaldeans.

10. They were educated for three years.

11. He gave to Daniel the name Belteshazzar; to Hananiah, Shadrach; to Mishael, Meshach; and to Azariah, Abed-Nego.

12. Daniel purposed in his heart that he would not defile himself with the portion of the king's delicacies or with the wine that he drank.

13. Daniel sought permission from the chief of the eunuchs, Ashpenaz.

14. He asked that for ten days, they be given vegetables to eat and water to drink. Then he was to compare their appearance with that of the young men who ate the portion of the king's delicacies to see if there was a difference. At the end of ten days, their features appeared better and fatter in flesh than all the young men who ate the portion of the king's delicacies. So they were allowed to continue eating that way.

15. God gave them knowledge and skill in all literature and wisdom and Daniel had understanding in all visions and dreams.

16. In all matters of wisdom and understanding about which the king examined them, he found them ten times better than all the magicians and astrologers who were in his entire realm.

17. Daniel served Nebuchadnezzar until the first year of King Cyrus (539 B.C.).

Chapter Two: Nebuchadnezzar's Dream

Read Daniel 2:1-45.

1. Nebuchadnezzar had his dreams in the second year of his reign in Babylon.
2. Magicians, astrologers, sorcerers, and the Chaldeans (wise men) were called to help the king.
3. They had to tell the king what he had dreamed and then interpret it.
4. If they failed to interpret his dream, they would be cut into pieces and their homes would be destroyed.
5. If they could interpret his dream, they would receive gifts, rewards, and great honor.
6. The king was furious and gave the command to destroy all the wise men of Babylon.
7. Daniel and his companions did not worship the idol.
8. Daniel went to his home and let his companions—Hananiah, Mishael, and Azariah—know what was happening. Together, they sought mercies from God to be able to tell the dream and interpret it.
9. The dream was revealed to Daniel in a night vision. So Daniel blessed and praised the God of heaven.
10. He told Arioch not to destroy the wise men of Babylon but to take him to the king so he could interpret his dream.
11. Daniel was able to tell him about the real God of heaven.
12. He wanted the king to know it was for the sake of all those he intended to destroy that the God of heaven revealed the dream.
13. He made sure God received the glory.
14. See Daniel 2:31-35.
15. The stone struck the image on its feet and then became a great mountain and filled the whole earth.

16. The iron, clay, bronze, silver, and gold were crushed together and became like chaff from the summer threshing floors. The wind carried them away so that no trace of them was found.

17. King Nebuchadnezzar represents the head of gold.

18. God gave Nebuchadnezzar his power.

19. The fourth kingdom is a kingdom that will break into pieces and crush all the other kingdoms.

20. Jesus is represented by the stone.

21. Nebuchadnezzar declared God is the God of gods, the Lord of kings, and a revealer of secrets.

22. He fell on his face, prostrate before Daniel, and commanded that they should present an offering and incense to him. He then promoted Daniel and gave him many great gifts. He also made him ruler over the whole province of Babylon and chief administrator over all the wise men of Babylon.

23. Shadrach, Meshach, and Abed-Nego were set in charge over the affairs of the province of Babylon.

Chapter Three: Into the Fiery Furnace

Read Daniel 3:1-30.

1. The image of gold was sixty cubits high and its width six cubits, which is approximately thirty metres high by three metres wide or ninety-eight feet high by nine feet wide.

2. He set it up in the plain of Dura in the province of Babylon.

3. The satraps, administrators, governors, counselors, treasurers, judges, magistrates, and all the officials of the provinces were to be present for the dedication of the idol.

4. There is nothing in the Bible to indicate that the statue was made in Nebuchadnezzar's image. In my opinion, I believe it is far more probable he was recreating the image of the statue he saw in his dream.

5. When the people heard the sound of the horn, flute, zither, lyre, harp, pipe and all kinds of music, they were commanded to fall down and worship the gold image.

6. Whoever did not fall down and worship the idol would be cast immediately into the midst of a fiery furnace.

7. Shadrach, Meshach, and Abed-Nego did not worship the idol.

8. They likely did not include Daniel because he was ruler over the whole province of Babylon and chief administrator over all the wise men of Babylon. He was essentially their boss. They also knew how much the king favoured him. Whereas, Shadrach, Meshach, and Abed-Nego were Daniel's administrators and possibly did not spend much time in the king's presence.

9. Nebuchadnezzar gave the men one choice: worship the image or be thrown into a scorching furnace. They told the king that God was able to deliver them from the fiery furnace and He would deliver them from the king's hand. However, if God chose not to save them, they still would not serve Nebuchadnezzar's gods nor would they worship the gold image he had set up.

10. They were killed by the flames of the furnace.

11. Nebuchadnezzar saw four men in the furnace rather than three.

12. He likened the fourth person to a son of the gods. Some translations mistranslate this to read Son of God. This is a Christian term, not a Jewish one, and is not found in the original text.

13. The hairs on their head were not singed nor were their garments affected and the smell of fire was not on them.

14. The king declared that any people, nation, or language that spoke anything amiss against the God of Shadrach, Meshach, and Abed-Nego would be cut in pieces and their houses made an ash heap.

Chapter Four: God is in Control

Read Daniel 4:1-37.

1. Nebuchadnezzar and Daniel wrote this chapter. It is believed the first part of this chapter was sent by Nebuchadnezzar to all the provinces to describe what had happened to him. The second part was written by Daniel in his own words. And the last part was written by the king. In other words, Daniel incorporated Nebuchadnezzar's confession into his book.
2. The chapter was written to all peoples, nations, and languages that dwell in all the earth.
3. It was written to give praise to God and to let the people know King Nebuchadnezzar now worshipped the God of the Jews.
4. Nebuchadnezzar called all the wise men of Babylon to interpret his dream. This would include the magicians, the conjurers, the Chaldeans, and the diviners. The verse suggests he still relied on the occult despite the fact that he professed belief in God.
5. Nebuchadnezzar called Daniel "Belteshazzar," which means "Bel protect him." Bel was one of the many gods whom the Babylonians worshipped.
6. King Nebuchadnezzar was the tree.
7. The tree was chopped down and destroyed, but its stump and roots were left in the earth. It had a band of iron and bronze around it and it (Nebuchadnezzar) would share with the beasts of the field and be wet with the dew of heaven until seven years had passed.
8. The king will be driven from his kingdom and dwell with the beasts of the field, where he will eat grass like oxen for seven years. In other words, he will go mad.

9. The king is sent to live in the field and descends into madness to show him that God rules in the kingdom of men and gives it to whomever He chooses.

10. Daniel advises the king to break away from his sins by being righteous and from his iniquities by showing mercy to the poor.

11. One year later the king was walking about the royal palace of Babylon, when he said, "Is not this great Babylon that I have built for a royal dwelling by my mighty power and for the honor of my majesty?" While he was still speaking, he heard a voice from heaven declare that his kingdom would depart from him for seven years. Within the hour Nebuchadnezzar went insane and was driven (most likely by angels) from his palace.

12. Nebuchadnezzar was cast out of his kingdom for seven years.

13. At the end of seven years, understanding and reason returned to Nebuchadnezzar and he acknowledged God as King.

Chapter Five: The Writing on the Wall

Read Daniel 5:1-31.

1. One thousand of his lords plus his wives and concubines were present for Belshazzar's feast.

2. Belshazzar gave the command to bring the gold and silver vessels that his father, Nebuchadnezzar, had taken from the Temple in Jerusalem so the king and his lords, wives, and concubines might drink from them.

3. They praised the gods of gold and silver, bronze and iron, wood and stone.

4. When the king saw the hand appear, his countenance changed, and his thoughts troubled him, so that the joints of his hips were loosened and his knees knocked against each

other. In other words, he was so scared he could barely stand up. We would say, "He was shaking in his boots."

5. Belshazzar cried aloud to bring in the astrologers, Chaldeans, and soothsayers. He said whoever could read the writing and explain its interpretation would be clothed with purple and have a chain of gold around his neck and be the third ruler in the kingdom.

6. The queen talked about Daniel's light, understanding, and wisdom: "Like the wisdom of the gods." She stressed that King Nebuchadnezzar made him chief of the magicians, astrologers, Chaldeans, and soothsayers. She said Daniel had an excellent spirit, knowledge, and understanding, that he could interpret dreams, solve riddles, and explain enigmas.

7. Daniel tells the king he has lifted himself up against the Lord of heaven, that he has knowingly taken the items from the Temple in Jerusalem, God's house, and used them to praise the gods of silver and gold, bronze and iron, wood and stone. He reminds him it is God who holds the king's breath in His hand and owns all his ways. Daniel tells the king he has not glorified the Lord.

8. This is the interpretation of each word written on the wall. MENE: God has numbered your kingdom and finished it. TEKEL: You have been weighed in the balances and found wanting. PERES: Your kingdom has been divided and given to the Medes and Persians.

9. Belshazzar's kingdom was given to Darius the Mede.

10. The king honoured Daniel by clothing him with purple, putting a chain of gold around his neck, and making a proclamation concerning him, that he should be the third ruler in the kingdom.

11. That very night Belshazzar was murdered.

Chapter Six: The Lion's Den

Read Daniel 6:1-28.

1. Darius set 120 governors (satraps) over the whole kingdom.
2. He set three presidents (overseers) over the satraps (governors).
3. Daniel was a president or overseer.
4. Daniel distinguished himself by his "excellent spirit."
5. The king thought about putting Daniel in charge of the whole realm.
6. The satraps and overseers tried to find grounds to accuse Daniel in regard to government affairs. But they could find no grounds or evidence of corruption because he was faithful and honest. No negligence or corruption was found in him.
7. They sought to attack Daniel's faith so he would be forced to either disobey God or the laws of the land. They did this by urging the king to establish a royal statute and make a firm decree that whoever prayed to any god or man other than the king should be cast into a den of lions. Once the king signed it, according to the laws of the Medes and Persians, it could not be revoked.
8. Daniel knew exactly what they had done and continued to pray three times a day in his chamber, knowing full well the satraps and overseers planned to "catch him" while he was praying.
9. The king was deeply distressed that he couldn't change his edict and he tried to find ways to rescue Daniel right up until the sun set.
10. The king believed Daniel's God would deliver him and told him so in Daniel 6:16, when he said, "Your God, whom you serve continually, He will deliver you."
11. The king went off to his palace and spent the night fasting. No entertainment was brought before him and he did not sleep.
12. The king woke early and went quickly to the lion's den, then called out to Daniel asking if God had saved him.

13. The king gave orders and they brought the men who had accused Daniel and cast them, their children, and their wives into the lions' den. The lions, whose mouths had been shut by God when Daniel was with them, overpowered them all before they even reached the bottom of the den and the lions crushed all their bones.

Chapter Seven: Strange Dreams

Read Daniel 7:1-28.

1. The main event or subject of this chapter is Daniel's dream about the four beasts.
2. The four beasts come from the sea.
3. The first beast was like a lion and had eagle's wings. These wings were plucked off and it was lifted up from the earth and made to stand on two feet like a man. A man's heart was given to it.
4. The statue was terrifying. Its head was of fine gold, its chest and arms of silver, its belly and thighs of bronze, its legs of iron, and its feet partly of iron and partly of clay. A stone was cut out without hands, which struck the image on its feet of iron and clay and broke them into pieces. Then the iron, clay, bronze, silver, and gold were crushed together and became like chaff. The wind carried them away so no trace of them was found. And the stone that struck the image became a great mountain and filled the whole earth.
5. King Nebuchadnezzar is the head of gold.
6. Both images represented King Nebuchadnezzar and his kingdom. Both were strong and powerful (represented by the lion and eagle in Daniel 7:4 and by the tree in Daniel 4:10-12). Both were removed from power (the eagle had its wings plucked and the tree was chopped down).
7. The second beast resembled a bear and it was raised up on one side. Three ribs were in its mouth, between its teeth.

8. The second beast was commanded to "arise and devour much meat."

9. The statue's breasts and arms were made of silver.

10. No

11. The next ruler of Babylon after Belshazzar was Darius the Mede.

12. The third beast looked like a leopard, which had four wings of a bird on its back. The beast also had four heads, and dominion was given to it.

13. The belly and thighs of the statue were made of bronze.

14. The third kingdom of bronze shall rule over all the earth.

15. The name of the third kingdom is Greece.

16. The fourth beast was dreadful, terrible, and extremely strong. It had huge iron teeth. It was devouring, breaking into pieces, and trampling the residue with its feet. It was different from all the beasts that were before it and it had ten horns.

17. The legs of the statue were made of iron, its feet partly of iron and partly of clay.

18. The fourth kingdom will break in pieces and crush all the other kingdoms.

19. This kingdom was different than all the others because it had ten horns.

Chapter Eight: The Ancient of Days

Verses covered are Revelation 4:1-10; Isaiah 6:1-3; Psalm 11:4; Psalm 47:8; Psalm 93:1-2; Psalm 103:19; Ezekiel 1:25-27; Daniel 7:9-10; Revelation 20:11.

1. God's throne resides in heaven. God is like a jasper stone and a sardius in appearance. The train of His robe fills the Temple. Seraphim stand above Him. There is a rainbow around His throne, like an emerald in appearance. God is everlasting. He is clothed with majesty and strength. He looks like a man, but from his waist up is the colour of

amber, with the appearance of fire all around and within. From his waist downward is the appearance of fire with brightness all around. His garment is as white as snow and the hair of His head is like pure wool. Heaven and Earth flee from His presence.

2. Seraphim stood above God, each with six wings. With two they covered their face, with two they covered their feet, and with two they flew. And one called out to another and said, "Holy, Holy, Holy, is the Lord of hosts, the whole earth is full of His glory."

3. There was a rainbow around God's throne, like an emerald in appearance. Around the throne were twenty-four thrones, and upon the thrones were twenty-four elders clothed in white garments, with golden crowns on their heads. His throne was high and lifted up. His throne was old and was like a sapphire stone. It appeared to be a flaming fire and it had wheels that were also a burning fire. A fiery stream issued before Him.

4. Peals of thunder came out of the throne.

5. God rules over all.

6. The fourth beast was dreadful, terrifying, and extremely strong. It had large iron teeth. It devoured, crushed, and trampled the remainder with its feet, and it was different from all the beasts that were before it because it had ten horns.

7. Three of the first horns were pulled out by the roots by the little horn.

8. The little horn uttered great boasts.

9. The beast was slain and its body was destroyed and given to the burning fire. The rest of the beasts had their dominion taken away, but an extension of life was granted to them for an appointed period of time.

10. One like the Son of Man was presented to the Ancient of Days. The Aramaic phrase *bar enash* means "human being." Most scholars believe it is Jesus who is presented.

11. The Son of Man was given authority, glory, and sovereign power so all nations and peoples of every language worshiped him.

12. His dominion is an everlasting dominion that will not pass away.

13. His kingdom is one that will never be destroyed.

14. Jesus has made us to be a kingdom and priests to serve His God and Father.

Chapter Ten: The Vision Interpreted

Read Daniel 7:15-28.

1. The four great beasts are four kings who arise out of the earth.

2. The saints of the Most High shall receive the kingdom and possess it forever.

3. Ten horns were on the fourth beast's head.

4. The ten horns come from the fourth beast, which is the Roman Empire.

5. Three kings are subdued.

6. He will speak pompous words against God. He will persecute the saints of God by changing the times and the law.

7. "Times, time and half a time" equals three and a half years.

8. His dominion is taken away and destroyed for all time.

9. All the kingdoms under the whole of heaven were given to the people, the saints of the Most High.

10. The kingdom will last forever.

Chapter Eleven: The Ram and the Goat

Read Daniel 8:1-27.

1. Daniel had his vision in the third year of the reign of King Belshazzar.
2. Three years had passed between Daniel's visions.
3. Daniel saw himself in Shushan, the citadel, which is in the province of Elam. He also saw that he was by the River Ulai. These are all in Iran.
4. A ram was standing by the river.
5. It had two horns.
6. The ram was pushing westward, northward, and southward.
7. The ram with two horns represented the kings of Media and Persia.
8. The male goat was the kingdom of Greece.
9. A large horn was between the goat's eyes, and it represented the first king, Alexander the Great.
10. The goat attacked the ram and broke his two horns.
11. When the large horn was broken, four other horns grew up in its place.

Chapter Twelve: The Big Reveal

Read Daniel 8:9-27.

1. The stars were mighty men and holy people. The word "mighty" in Hebrew is `atsuwm. It is an adjective and is translated as "vast, numerous or strong." The word "holy" (qadowsh) is also an adjective and translates as "saints." So the people who are destroyed are described as vast, numerous, strong, and holy. In other words, they are the Jewish people.
2. The little horn that grew exceedingly great stretched towards the south, the east, and the Glorious Land (Israel).
3. The Temple would lie desolate and the sacrifices would cease for 2,300 evenings and mornings.
4. The angel Gabriel helped Daniel understand the vision.
5. The ram with two horns were the kings of Media and Persia.

6. The shaggy goat was the kingdom of Greece and the large horn represented Alexander the Great.

7. The four kingdoms shall come from the Greek Empire.

8. He will oppose the Prince of Princes. Some have taken this to mean he will stand up against Jesus or the archangel Michael. However, the word Prince (*sar*) is also used in reference to the priests (in particular the high priest) of the Jewish Temple.

9. He will be stopped without human means. In other words, God will intervene and put an end to him.

10. Daniel was ordered to seal up the vision.

Chapter Thirteen: Seventy Weeks

Read Daniel 9:1-19.

1. This chapter takes place in the first year of Darius the son of Ahasuerus. This would be Darius the Mede, not Darius the Great.

2. Daniel observed through the books that the exile of the Jews was in line with the prophecy given by the prophet Jeremiah (Jeremiah 25:1-19).

3. Jerusalem would lie desolate and the Jewish nation would serve the king of Babylon for seventy years.

4. Daniel wept and prayed, confessing his nation's guilt and sin toward God, and sought His forgiveness.

5. Daniel confessed his people had done wickedly and rebelled by departing from God's precepts and judgments. They were unfaithful and sinned against God. He also confessed they did not pay attention to the prophets God had sent them.

Chapter Fourteen: Who Issued the Decree?

Read Daniel 9:20-27.

1. Gabriel came to Daniel while he was still praying on behalf of his people.
2. Gabriel came to give Daniel insight and understanding.
3. The order was given to Gabriel to go to Daniel the moment Daniel started praying.
4. He was highly esteemed by God.
5. Seventy weeks were decreed (490 years) for Daniel's people and Jerusalem.
6. The seventy weeks would be to finish the transgression, make an end to sin, make atonement for iniquity, bring in everlasting righteousness, seal up vision and prophecy, and anoint the Most Holy Place.

Chapter Sixteen: Is it Past or is it Future?

Read Daniel 9:26-27

1. The anointed one (Messiah) will be cut off and have nothing.
2. In the JPS version the anointed one will be cut off and be no more.
3. The people of the prince who is to come will destroy the city and the sanctuary.
4. The NASB implies that the city (Jerusalem) and the Temple will be destroyed (come with a flood), while the JPS implies that the anointed one's end will come with a flood (be destroyed).
5. The prince agrees to make a firm covenant with the Jews for one week (seven years).
6. Midway through the covenant, the prince breaks it and puts a stop to the sacrifices and offerings. In addition, he sets up an abomination of desolation.

Chapter Seventeen: Unseen Forces

Read Daniel 10:1-21

1. Cyrus, king of Persia, was reigning.
2. Daniel mourned for three weeks after his vision.
3. Daniel saw a certain man dressed in linen whose waist was girded with a belt of pure gold of Uphaz. His body also was like beryl. His face had the appearance of lightning and his eyes were like flaming torches. His arms and feet were like the gleam of polished bronze, and the sound of his words was like the sound of a tumult.
4. It would appear that this particular being was not Gabriel, due to the reaction Daniel had upon seeing him. Daniel's strength left him and he turned deathly pale and fainted, as it says in Daniel 10:8-9.
5. A great dread fell on the men with Daniel and they ran away to hide themselves.
6. The angel called Daniel a man of high esteem.
7. The angel came to Daniel in response to his words of confession and because he humbled himself before God (see Daniel 9).
8. Daniel was speechless.

Chapter Eighteen: The Kings of the North and South (Part 1)

Read Daniel 11:1-35

1. The angel came to be an encouragement and protection to Darius the Mede.
2. Three more kings would arise in Persia.
3. The fourth king of Persia would gain far more riches than all of them.
4. After he becomes strong through his riches, he rouses the whole empire against the realm of Greece.
5. After the fourth king of Persia, a mighty king arose. He ruled with great authority and did as he pleased. His kingdom was broken up and parceled out toward the four points of the compass.

6. His kingdom did not go to his own descendants but was given to others.
7. The king of the south offers his daughter in marriage to the king of the north in order to form an alliance between the two kingdoms.
8. The peace between the two nations does not last.

Chapter Nineteen: The Kings of the North and South (Part 2)

Read Daniel 11:10-19.

1. The king of the north's sons banded together and mobilized an army to attack the king of the south. One of the sons managed to take his forces right up to the fortress of the king of the south. This enraged the king of the south, who went out to fight the king of the north. But the king of the north raised an even greater multitude (army). However, it was given into the hands of the king of the south.
2. The king of the south does not prevail because the king of the north will again raise a greater multitude, and after an interval of some years, he will press on with a great army and much equipment to defeat him.
3. The term "violent ones" quoted in Daniel 11:14 is translated as "robber or murderer" from the Hebrew word *pĕriyts*. They sought to exalt themselves by fulfilling their vision of being free from the king of the south, but they failed. History would reveal that the leaders of the Jewish community would later support the king of the north, Antiochus III, by welcoming him into Jerusalem. Unfortunately, when Antiochus Epiphanes IV gained control of the throne, the Jews would soon regret welcoming the king of the north into Jerusalem.
4. The King of the north captures many but is stopped.

Chapter Twenty: The Kings of the North and South (Part 3)

Read Daniel 11:20-30.

1. He sent someone to oppress the Jews (quite possibly by taxing the Temple), but within a few days, he was shattered—or was no more.
2. He came in a time of peace and seized the kingdom through intrigue and deception.
3. After an alliance is made with him, the king of the north will practice deception and he will go up and gain power with a small force of people.
4. He distributes plunder, booty, and possessions among the people to gain their trust.
5. The king of the south fails and the king of the north prevails again.
6. Both kings' hearts are intent on evil and they lie to each other while at the same table.
7. He comes against the king of the south one more time, but this time the forces of Rome are against him and send ships from Kittim to destroy him.
8. He shows regard for those Jews who forsake the covenant.

Chapter Twenty-One: The Kings of the North and South (Part 4)

Read Daniel 11:31-45.

1. They desecrate the sanctuary fortress and do away with the regular sacrifice.
2. They set up the abomination of desolation (an idol).
3. By smooth and deceitful words, he encouraged people to turn to godlessness and act wickedly toward the Jewish people (the covenant people) and toward God.
4. Those faithful to God display strength and take action against the king of the north.

5. Those who go up against the king of the north fall by sword and by flame, by captivity and by plunder for many days.

6. The new king does as he pleases, and he exalts and magnifies himself above every god and will speak monstrous things against the God of gods. This continues until "the indignation is finished" (in other words, for as long as God will allow it).

7. The king honours the god of fortresses through gold, silver, costly stones, and treasures. He continues to build fortresses and attempts to take fortresses already built by others.

8. He gives great honour to those who acknowledge him and causes them to rule over the many and parcels out land for a price.

9. The countries rescued out of his hand are Edom, Moab, and the foremost of the sons of Ammon (modern day Jordan).

10. He gains control over the hidden treasures of gold and silver and over all the precious things of Egypt.

11. The Libyans and Ethiopians follow this king.

12. The king goes forth and annihilates many.

13. He dies with no one to help him.

Chapter Twenty-Two: A Look into the Future?

Read Daniel 12:1-13.

1. The archangel Michael will stand up during the times of Herod/the Roman Empire.

2. Michael stands watch over the Jews.

3. Everyone who is found written in the Book shall be rescued.

4. Those who sleep will awake, some to everlasting life, others to everlasting contempt. The word "sleep" is a metaphor for death. This could be a literal resurrection from the dead or it could mean that many wake from a spiritual slumber that results in their being renewed (everlasting life) or condemned (everlasting contempt).

5. Those who are wise or have insight shall shine like the brightness of the firmament and turn many to righteousness like the stars forever and ever.

6. Daniel is to seal his book until the time of the end.

7. While the book is sealed, many will run to and fro and knowledge will increase.

8. He was told it would be for a time, times, and half a time; and when the power of the holy people had been completely shattered, all these things would be finished.

9. The holy people are the righteous of Israel, who have not forsaken God, those Jews who held onto their beliefs and their faith in God. This could be in reference to the Maccabean revolt.

10. The wicked will not understand what is happening. Only those with insight or who are wise will understand what is happening. How do we gain insight and wisdom? Through knowledge of the Word of God.

ABOUT THE AUTHOR

Laura J. Davis is a former singer/songwriter who took to writing full-time after emergency surgery caused the loss of her singing voice. Her singing career had lasted for thirty years. Her first book, *Come to Me*, won a Reader's Favorite Award. In 2013, her Bible study *Learning from the Master, Living a Surrendered Life*, was featured in *Book Fun Magazine* as the non-fiction book of the month first place winner. She has had stories featured in *Chicken Soup for the Soul Married Life* and *Chicken Soup for the Soul the Dating Game*. Her last book, *He Who Has an Ear*, is a look at who the seven churches of Revelation are today.

Laura is a trained Precept Ministries teacher and has a passion for digging into Scripture. You can connect with Laura through her website at www.laurajdavis.com; on Twitter at www.twitter.com/laurajeandavis; and on Facebook at www.facebook.com/LauraDavis. If you liked this book please consider leaving a review on Amazon.com or Amazon.ca.

Want to continue digging deeper into the Scriptures? The next book in the Digging Deeper series will be a study of Revelation. Sign up to Laura's mailing list to be the first to know when it's coming out http://eepurl.com/EGzJr.

BIBLIOGRAPHY

Briney, A. (n.d.). The Ottoman Empire. Retrieved 03 02, 2015, from About.com: http://geography.about.com/od/historyofgeography/a/The-Ottoman-Empire.htm

Chabad Contributors. (n.d.). Chanukah FAQ's - Chanukah Basics - Chanukah, Hanukkah. Retrieved 02 02, 2016, from Chabad.org: http://www.chabad.org/holidays/chanukah/article_cdo/aid/605036/jewish/Chanukah-FAQs.htm

Editors of Encyclopaedia Brittanica. (n.d.). Belshazzar King of Babylonia. Retrieved 01 28, 2016, from Encyclopaedia Brittanica: http://www.britannica.com/biography/Belshazzar

Editors of the Encyclopedia Brittanica. (n.d.). Ptolemy III Euergetes, Macedonian king of Egypt. Retrieved 01 28, 2016, from Encyclopedia Brittanica: http://www.britannica.com/biography/Ptolemy-III-Euergetes

Eric Lyons, M. (n.d.). Alleged Discrepancies. Retrieved 05 20, 2015, from Apologetics Press: https://www.apologeticspress.org/apcontent.aspx?category=6&article=740

Eyewitness to History. (n.d.). The Death of Alexander the Great, 323 B.C. Retrieved 04 12, 2015, from Eyewitness to History: http://www.eyewitnesstohistory.com/alexanderdeath.htm

Flavius, J. (78 C.E.). The History of the Destruction of Jerusalem (The War of the Jews). Rome.

Flavius, J. (n.d.). The Romans Destroy the Temple at Jerusalem, 70 AD. Retrieved 08 23, 2015, from Eyewitness to History: http://eyewitnesstohistory.com/jewishtemple.htm

Flavius, J. (n.d.). The Wars of the Jews or the History of the Destruction of Jerusalem. Retrieved 04 12, 2015, from Sacred Texts: War, 1: 2; Whiston, V3: 11

Flavius, J. (n.d.). The Works of Flavius Josephus. Retrieved 01 28, 2016, from Perseus Digital Library: http://www.perseus.tufts.edu/hopper/text?doc=Perseus%3Atext%3A1999.01.0146%3Abook%3D14%3Awhiston+chapter%3D4%3Awhiston+section%3D4#note-link1

Heinen, H. (n.d.). Ptolemy II Philadelphus, Macedonian king of Egypt. Retrieved 11 05, 2015, from Encyclopedia Brittanica: http://www.britannica.com/biography/Ptolemy-II-Philadelphus

House of One. (2011). Idea. Retrieved 03 13, 2015, from House of One: http://house-of-one.org/en/idea

Huie, B. T. (2015, 12). Daniel 11 - Prophecy Fulfilled. Retrieved 05 02, 2015, from Here a Little, There a Little: http://www.herealittletherealittle.net/index.cfm?page_name=Daniel11

Luther, M. (n.d.). Smalcald Articles. Retrieved 01 31, 2016, from Book of Concord: http://bookofconcord.org/smalcald.php#article4

Lynfield, B. (2009, 12 03). Arab Scholar Blasted Over Temple Mount. Retrieved 01 28, 2016, from The Jewish Chronicle: http://www.thejc.com/news/israel-news/24589/arab-scholar-blasted-over-temple-mount

Lyons, E. (2005). Kingly Chronology in the Book of Ezra. Retrieved 03 02, 2015, from Apologetics Press: http://www.apologeticspress.org/apcontent.aspx?category=6&article=740

New World Encylopedia Contributors. (2012, 10 09). Antiochus IV Epiphanes. Retrieved 01 28, 2016, from New World Encyclopedia: http://www.newworldencyclopedia.org/entry/Antiochus_IV_Epiphanes

Polybius. (n.d.). Battle of Raphia. Retrieved 02 05, 2015, from Wikepedia: https://en.wikipedia.org/wiki/Battle_of_Raphia

Rider, D. (2015, 05 13). City Hall. Retrieved 05 14, 2015, from The Star: http://www.thestar.com/news/city_hall/2015/05/13/o-canada-nixed-by-richmond-hill-town-council.html

Seeking Truth Contributors. (n.d.). Europe in Bible Prophecy. Retrieved 05 16, 2015, from Seeking Truth: http://www.seekingtruth.co.uk/europe.htm

Socrates. (430 BC). Musings. Ahtens: Self Published.

Sproul, R. (n.d.). Is the Reformation Over? Retrieved 01 28, 2015, from Ligonier Ministries: http://www.ligonier.org/learn/articles/reformation-over/

Trueman, C. (2015, 03 16). The Fall of Ancient Rome. Retrieved 12 23, 2015, from The History Learning Site: "The fall of Ancient Rome". HistoryLearningCite.co.uk. 2006. Web.

Turner, R. (n.d.). Reasons Why the Apocrypha Does Not Belong in the Bible. Retrieved from CARM - Christian Apologetics and Research Ministry: https://carm.org/why-apocrypha-not-in-bible

United With Israel. (2011, 06 21). Is Jerusalem Holy for Muslims as for Jews? Retrieved 01 28, 2016, from United With Isrârel:
http://unitedwithisrael.org/jerusalem-holy-for-jews/

Unknown. (n.d.). The European Flag. Retrieved 02 03, 2015, from European Union: http://europa.eu/about-eu/basic-information/symbols/flag/index_en.htm

Westminster Assembly. (n.d.). Of the Church. Retrieved 01 31, 2016, from Center for Reformed Theology and Apologetics:
http://www.reformed.org/documents/wcf_with_proofs/

Wikipedia contributors. (n.d.). Alexander the Great. Retrieved 01 28, 2016, from Wikipedia:
https://en.wikipedia.org/wiki/Alexander_the_Great#Division_of_the_empire

Wikipedia Contributors. (n.d.). Antiochus II Theos. Retrieved 05 13, 2015, from Wikipedia: https://en.wikipedia.org/wiki/Antiochus_II_Theos

Wikipedia Contributors. (n.d.). Canon of the Kings. Retrieved from Wikipedia: https://en.wikipedia.org/wiki/Canon_of_Kings

Wikipedia Contributors. (n.d.). Ptolemy III Eugergetes. Retrieved 01 28, 2016, from Wikipedia: https://en.wikipedia.org/wiki/Ptolemy_III_Euergetes

Young, D. G. (2005). The Roots of the Israeli-Arab Conflict. Retrieved 03 02, 2015, from Focus on Jerusalem:
http://www.focusonjerusalem.com/TheRootsoftheIsraeli-ArabConflict.htm

NOTES

[1] *http://www.britannica.com/biography/Belshazzar*

[2] *http://bookofconcord.org/smalcald.php#article4*

[3] *http://www.freepres.org/westminster.htm*

[4] *http://www.ligonier.org/learn/articles/reformation-over/*

[5] *http://www.seekingtruth.co.uk/europe.htm*

[6] *http://europa.eu/about-eu/basic-information/symbols/flag/index_en.htm*

[7] *http://house-of-one.org/en*

[8] *http://geography.about.com/od/historyofgeography/a/The-Ottoman-Empire.htm*

[9] *http://www.focusonjerusalem.com/TheRootsoftheIsraeli-AraB.C.onflict.htm*

[10] *"The fall of Ancient Rome". HistoryLearningCite.co.uk. 2006. Web.*

[11] *http://www.eyewitnesstohistory.com/alexanderdeath.htm*

[12] *http://www.newworldencyclopedia.org/entry/Antiochus_IV_Epiphanes*

[13] *http://www.newworldencyclopedia.org/entry/Antiochus_IV_Epiphanes*

[14] *Josephus, Antiquities of the Jews 14:70-71*

[15] *The Romans Destroy the Temple at Jerusalem, 70 AD, EyeWitness to History, www.eyewitnesstohistory.com (2005)*

[16] *http://tinyurl.com/26e5jpc*

[17] *Toronto Star, http://tinyurl.com/l2dvk3k*

[18] *https://en.wikipedia.org/wiki/Canon_of_Kings*

[19] *http://www.apologeticspress.org/apcontent.aspx?category=6&article=740*

[20] *History of the Destruction of Jerusalem, Josephus Flavius, http://sacred-texts.com/jud/josephus/war-1.htm*

[21] *http://www.thejc.com/news/israel-news/24589/arab-scholar-blasted-over-Temple-mount*

[22] *http://unitedwithisrael.org/jerusalem-holy-for-jews/*

[23] *https://www.youtube.com/watch?v=7-JKE_HPHSo*

[24] *https://en.wikipedia.org/wiki/Alexander_the_Great#Division_of_the_empire*

[25] *Encyclopedia Britannica, http://tinyurl.com/lujh8qt*

[26] *http://www.herealittletherealittle.net/index.cfm?page_name=Daniel11*

[27] *http://en.wikipedia.org/wiki/Antiochus_II_Theos*

[28] *http://www.britannica.com/biography/Ptolemy-III-Euergetes*

[29] *https://en.wikipedia.org/wiki/Ptolemy_III_Euergetes*

[30] *http://en.wikipedia.org/wiki/Battle_of_Raphia*

[31] *Polybius V.65 and V.79-87*

[32] *https://carm.org/why-apocrypha-not-in-bible*

[33] *https://en.wikipedia.org/wiki/Ptolemy_IV_Philopator*

[34] *Syrian Wars, Wikipedia, http://tinyurl.com/ohjt9kx*

[35] *Syrian Wars, Wikipedia, http://tinyurl.com/ohjt9kx*

[36] *Jewish Antiquities, 12.3.3*

[37] *Battle of Panium, Wikipedia, http://en.wikipedia.org/wiki/Battle_of_Panium*

[38] *Syrian Wars, Wikipedia, http://tinyurl.com/ohjt9kx*

Cleopatra I, Wikipedia, http://en.wikipedia.org/wiki/Cleopatra_I_Syra

[39] Cleopatra I, Wikipedia, http://en.wikipedia.org/wiki/Cleopatra_I_Syra
[40] https://en.wikipedia.org/wiki/Antiochus_III_the_Great
[41] Battle of Magnesia, Wikipedia,
http://en.wikipedia.org/wiki/Battle_of_Magnesia
[42] Antiochus III, Wikipedia, http://en.wikipedia.org/wiki/antiochus_III-the_Great
[43] http://en.wikipedia.org/wiki/Seleucus_IV_Philopator
[44] Sixth Syrian War, Wikipedia, http://tinyurl.com/nk2pbra
[45] Sixth Syrian War, Wikipedia, http://tinyurl.com/nk2pbra
[46] Jason (High priest, Wikipedia,
http://en.wikipedia.org/wiki/Jason_%28high_priest%29
[47] Seleucid Empire, Wikipedia, http://en.wikipedia.org/wiki/Seleucid_Empire
[48] Seleucid Empire, Wikipedia, http://en.wikipedia.org/wiki/Seleucid_Empire
[49] Herod the Great, Wikipedia, http://en.wikipedia.org/wiki/Herod_the_Great
[50] Herod the Great, Jewish Encyclopedia, http://tinyurl.com/pqegdae
[51] http://www.livius.org/he-hg/herodians/herod_the_great02.html
[52] https://www.jewishvirtuallibrary.org/jsource/Judaism/revolt.html
[53] Jewish Virtual Library, http://tinyurl.com/kd6cqan

9 780973 202212